PR FOR **ANYONE**™

PR FOR ANYONE™

100+ Affordable Ways to Easily Create Buzz for Your Business

Christina Daves

NEW YORK

PR FOR ANYONE™
100+ Affordable Ways to Easily Create Buzz for Your Business

Published in New York, New York, by Morgan James Publishing. Morgan James and The Entrepreneurial Publisher are trademarks of Morgan James, LLC.
www.MorganJamesPublishing.com

The Morgan James Speakers Group can bring authors to your live event. For more information or to book an event visit The Morgan James Speakers Group at www.TheMorganJamesSpeakersGroup.com.

FREE eBook edition for your
existing eReader with purchase

PRINT NAME ABOVE

For more information,
instructions, restrictions, and
to register your copy, go to
www.bitlit.ca/readers/register
or use your QR Reader to scan
the barcode:

ISBN 978-1-63047-033-3 paperback
ISBN 978-1-63047-034-0 eBook
ISBN 978-1-63047-036-4 hardcover
Library of Congress Control Number:
2013955195

Cover Design by:
Ted Angel
www.tedangel.com

Interior Design by:
Bonnie Bushman
bonnie@caboodlegraphics.com

In an effort to support local communities, raise awareness and funds, Morgan James Publishing donates a percentage of all book sales for the life of each book to Habitat for Humanity Peninsula and Greater Williamsburg.

Get involved today, visit
www.MorganJamesBuilds.com.

Habitat
for Humanity®
Peninsula and
Greater Williamsburg
Building Partner

To my incredible husband, Steve, who loves and supports me every step of the way—even when I see a new shiny penny. Nothing I do would be possible without you.

To my amazing kids, Justin and Megan, without whom, life would be meaningless.

Special thanks to everyone who contributed expertise or a unique story for this book. Sharing your knowledge is an invaluable gift you are providing readers. Thank you for being a part of this incredible journey!

Table of Contents

Shout It From the Rooftops 18

Your Message In a Bottle 27

We Want YOU! 44

Becoming Print-worthy — 60

Foreword

As a 37-year veteran of the PR industry, I know first-hand the struggles entrepreneurs and small business owners face needing to gain exposure, but not having the budget to carryout a full-fledged publicity campaign. Nothing is more effective in gaining exposure than free media placement, however, most business owners have no idea how to even start. *PR for Anyone™ 100+ Affordable Ways to Easily Create Buzz for You and Your Business* provides invaluable resources and tips for business owners to easily generate their own publicity.

Author, Christina Daves, shares her journey of launching a business and her quest for gaining exposure for a new product concept. Not having a budget for a publicist and without any experience in the industry, she managed to teach herself successful formulas that led to consistent media exposure. In this book, she teaches you how she handled her own publicity and achieved unprecedented success appearing in over 50 media outlets in less than one year. Christina put

PR for Anyone™ together in a format of easy-to-read tips to simplify gaining and using the knowledge she shares. She also enlists the resources of people in the media to share their tips to continue helping the reader navigate the waters of publicity and learn about what it is the media wants to see.

What I love about *PR for Anyone*™ is that it is written from the perspective of the small business owner. I was in the PR industry. It was my job to create publicity campaigns and gain exposure for my clients. But Christina shows you how it can be done in-house, affordably, and effectively by following her tips and recommendations. As an industry professional, I can put value on what she shares with the reader and attest to the fact that these systems will work if implemented. Bottom line, it's all about building relationships and Christina shows you how to do that with people in the media and how to continue to gain exposure for your business.

Welcome to the wonderful world of PR and congratulations on the success that is sure to come by reading and implementing what Christina has shared with you.

—**Rick Frishman,** Founder of Planned TV Arts
(now called Media Connect)

You're Off To Great Places! Today is Your Day!

—Dr. Seuss

INTRODUCTION

A.K.A. What Do I Know?

"There's no faux fur in China," my so-called retail expert advisor informed me.

Let's call him Richard. I hired Richard to help me manufacture and market my invention—accessories to make ugly medical boots fashion-forward and fun.

While some of my designs specified using faux fur, Richard's promises were the only fake items he delivered, reeling me in with his big-box name-dropping and personal charm.

He was supposed to make my dreams of bringing these uplifting accessories to the injured a reality by overseeing the manufacturing process and getting them placed in retail outlets.

I laughed. Surely he was joking. When he didn't laugh with me, I realized I had made a horrible mistake in paying this man $27,000. This man who expected me to believe China was in the midst of some economic crisis resulting in a national faux fur shortage.

Despite my bad hiring decision and complete lack of manufacturing knowledge, I was able to procure the furry inventory on my own. But there I was with over 50,000 pieces sitting in a fulfillment house ready to ship to anyone who wanted to buy and wondering to myself, *How in the world am I going to let people know about this product?* I was literally out of money and had no means to pay a public relations firm. How was anyone going to buy something they didn't even know existed?

I was in the dubious position of having a first-of-its-kind product with no easy way to share it with the world.

Unfortunately, hiring a PR firm at $1,500 to as much as $10,000 per month with a six-month minimum, and no guarantees of placement, is just too far out of reach for most of us. Public relations or PR, however, is a vital component for increasing sales, gaining credibility, and getting new customers. Most small businesses, including mine, are on tight budgets and have to decide where to spend money to grow. So I ended up handling my own PR—all of it.

We all wish we could hire the infamous movie character, Jerry Maguire, of *Show Me the Money!* fame to handle our PR. Nowadays, however, PR is a task that is being brought in-house by many companies either with someone on-staff or even the business owner handling it themselves. The big question becomes whether or not you or someone in your office can manage the PR for your business and be as effective as a public relations firm?

Any publicity you receive gives you instant credibility. There is the presumption that if you are covered by the media, you must be good at what you do. So the question is not whether you need PR, but how to obtain it most cost-effectively. For many of us, it becomes a "do-it-yourself" project, which really can be easier than it sounds.

While a PR firm you hire has insider contacts in the industry that they've already established, there is absolutely no reason you can't find your own media contacts and start building your own relationships. You can become a go-to expert in your industry or just land some great press coverage on your business, product, or service starting from scratch and all by yourself.

My friends call me "The Resourceful One" because I'm really good at researching and finding solutions. So I set out to learn everything I possibly could about public relations and how to gain media exposure.

Apparently I'm a quick study because I appeared in over fifty media outlets in one year, including nationally syndicated shows such as the *Steve Harvey Show* and *Dr. Oz,* as well as local *FOX, NBC,* and *CBS* affiliates, the *Washington Post, Parenting Magazine*, and many others—all in the first year of business!

I conducted countless hours of research on the Internet, listened to every *How to Gain Media Exposure* podcast I could find, and read every book I could get my hands on. I also attended a speed-dating format event with actual members of the media, which was great for learning how to become more comfortable talking to producers and reporters.

In fact, the best lesson I learned is that the people in the media are no different from us. Their job is to book guests or tell stories, and your job is to provide them with great content. They need us as much as we need them, maybe more. Connect with them and start building relationships so you become their go-to person in your area of expertise.

Now you know that it *can* be done, but you're probably wondering, *How much time is this going to take?* When I started, it took tons of time, but I've done all of that legwork for you. I've figured out the hard way what works and what doesn't, and I am sharing all of that information with you.

Some days I spend as little as fifteen minutes on PR and some days more. It's all about scheduling when you are going to work on it, and we'll get into that in more detail throughout the book. My suggestion is to start out dedicating about an hour a day to PR and you should start seeing results soon.

What I have done for you in this book is summarized all of my research and experience into easy tips for you to use to start generating your own publicity. Not only am I giving you my tips, but I also reached out to industry experts who have provided suggestions as well.

I am living proof that anyone can learn the basics of do-it-yourself PR, develop a personal plan, build relationships, and get great results! So put on your PR hat and get ready for some strategies that will allow you to create an effective PR campaign.

And I will bet you all the faux fur in China you can do it!

You Have to
Start Somewhere

ou know you've got a great business, even a superior business. But it's your competitor who is always hogging the spotlight, gaining the media exposure, the leads, and the customers.

You fantasize about what you would say if only you could shove them aside and tell the world how incredible you are. How you would wow them with your knowledge, dazzle them with your product, or simply share the logical reasons why your business is the best. In reality though, you're hunched over your laptop, daydreaming, wondering where to even start?

I hear it all the time: *I don't even know the first thing when it comes to PR.* Guess what? I didn't either. Now that I do, I'm going to share it all with you, and even include tips from industry experts.

At first, getting publicity seems elusive, even scary. I assure you this initial fear-of-the-unknown will pass quickly, especially once you start seeing results.

So relax. And let's get started.

You may not think these first tips relate to public relations, but they are absolutely crucial in building your overall image, brand, and ultimately, your PR.

Anything that represents you or your company is vital to your PR efforts. You must be professional, expert-worthy, and someone the media would want to share with their audience.

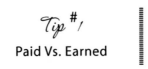

Tip #1

Paid Vs. Earned

Publicity is absolutely critical. A good PR story is infinitely more effective than a front page ad.

—Richard Branson

To start, PR and advertising are not the same thing.

Advertising is something for which you pay, and you get to control the message. So, you are paying to tell people what you want them to hear. There is often less credibility with advertising because everyone knows you paid for it.

PR is free, but you don't get to control what someone else conveys about you. You provide information in a press release or in an interview, then see what someone else has to say about you. The upside to PR, besides being free, is that it provides credibility. It's not you talking about you. It's someone else talking about you, and that makes it more believable. PR is essentially a third-party endorsement of you or your company, otherwise known in the public relations industry as "earned media."

The potential downside is a journalist who doesn't see things the way you do, and writes something not favorable. That actually happened to me very early on. A top blog site wrote about my products but didn't like them and said I had, "tween-meets-Michaels" designs. Ouch! Kick in the stomach with that review. Ironically, that post has led to thousands of dollars in sales. (Thank you to Google Analytics for showing from where sales are generated.) And the good news, that is the only bad review I've ever gotten.

Tip #2

What's in a Name?

What's in a name? That which we call a rose by any other name would smell as sweet.

—William Shakespeare

You absolutely must own your business domain name. If someone else already has it, reconsider the name of your business. There are variations you can use. However, I recommend against using a hyphenated domain name, or a name with an extension such as, LLC. It's too complicated and makes it difficult to differentiate yourself.

If you do decide to go the hyphen or extension route, be certain that the other website using your actual business domain name is one you would be okay with your customers or the media visiting. Odds are, at some point, they will land on that page inadvertently. If it's a direct competitor or someone who sells something that may be offensive, you should reconsider.

There are, however, unique ways to use your business name in a domain that can be effective. When I owned a brick and mortar store, Details for the Home, we tried to secure the domain, www.detailsforthehome.com. Someone had already purchased it, but they weren't using it. Since they were not in direct competition with us, and since we were a store, we opted to use www.shopatdetails.com, which worked for what we were doing.

Next, ask yourself if your domain name is easy to remember? If not, find one that is. Remember to make sure it's pertinent to your business as we did with Details using "shop at." Even if you're already doing business with an overly complicated name, just forward the new, easy-to-remember domain name to your existing website. This way, nothing changes except the odds that you'll gain more visitors.

When I started my current company, I loved the name my friends helped me come up with, CastMedic Designs. It was a perfect description of the product. It left room to expand the line. Best of all, it's my initials, "CMD." Perfect, right? Well, not so much.

Over time and with increased media appearances, I realized it was in fact, a terrible name! It's hard to remember, difficult to say, and even harder to spell. I cringed when I watched the recording of my appearance on the *Steve Harvey Show,* as he awkwardly pronounced my business name. CastMedic Designs doesn't exactly roll off the tongue.

I now own the domain, www.healinstyle.com. It's perfect for TV, radio, or just in conversation. It's memorable and I have it set up to forward to www.castmedicdesigns.com. This way, I didn't lose any online credibility already established with the original domain.

MY FAVORITE TIP
Don't forget variations and misspellings of your domain name. For example, I also own the domain, www. heelinstyle.com, which is also forwarded to the main CastMedic Designs website. Cover all of your bases with possible spelling issues. You want people to find you.

Tip #3
Do I Have a Deal For You!

The way to wealth depends on just two words, industry and frugality.

—Benjamin Franklin

An excellent place to search for domain names is Go Daddy at www.godaddy.com.

Before you start searching and purchasing, let me share a little money-saving secret with you. Go to Google and enter "Go Daddy coupon." Nine times out of ten, you will find a coupon for a $2.49 to $3.99 annual fee for a domain name.

The coupons are usually limited to one per month. Using this discount, however, allows you to stockpile domain names pertinent to your business, at a low price.

MY FAVORITE TIP
I've had great luck going to my favorite discount and coupon site, RetailMeNot at www.retailmenot.com and finding Go Daddy deals. Most of the domains I own, I purchased for under $5.00 for the first year.

Tip # 4
Your Online Presence = Your Calling Card

Quality is not an act, it is a habit.

—**Aristotle**

Have you ever gone to a website and thought, "*Ugh,*" or tried to find a business online that didn't have a website?

In today's age of immediate access to everything, not having a business website negatively affects your credibility. People want to see with whom they're dealing and a website is the best way to do that.

As a consumer, if you're deciding between two places to buy something, or which company to hire, odds are, you are going to choose the one that presents itself better, the one that looks more professional.

You can find free website builders at www.top10bestwebsitebuilders.com, so there is no reason for you not to have a website.

There are also sites such as, www.elance.com, www.odesk.com, and www.99designs.com where graphic design freelancers bid on winning your business. You join for free, submit a proposal for a job, and freelancers send their qualifications along with their bid. Then you simply hire the one you think is the best freelancer for your job. You escrow money for the project through the online company and don't pay until you are satisfied.

Don't discount Craig's List, www.craigslist.com. There are a great many talented people posting freelance services there as well.

The single most important piece of advice in this book, and the best thing you can do for your PR, is to make sure the face of your business screams "professional" and "expert"! Let the world know that you are the best.

When you submit a story idea or an expert request to a journalist, the first thing they will likely do is visit your website and social media pages. They need to make sure you are someone they should write about or source. If you don't have a website or it's not projecting professionalism, they are not going to want to reference it in their project.

It's also important to make sure your Facebook and Twitter cover pages are created professionally. These graphics can be done economically at www.fiverr.com.

Remember, every part of your online presence is representing you. So make yourself look good!

MY FAVORITE TIP

www.fiverr.com. **This site is the greatest ever! People will do anything for $5.00. Yes, $5.00. Search the site and find a portfolio you like and request a job. You pay $5.00 and they deliver whatever you ordered. I had PR for Anyone's Facebook** (www.facebook.com/PRforAnyone) **and Twitter** (www.twitter.com/PRforAnyone) **covers both created on Fiverr.**

Tip #5

Your Mug Is Your Money

A picture is worth a thousand words.

—Napoleon Bonaparte

Just like your online presence, your photographs represent you and your business. I encourage you to invest in high-resolution, high-quality photographs for publicity. An immediate media opportunity could present itself and require high-resolution photos. Even for a blog, you want to represent your product and your company with good, high-quality images. This type of photography is not expensive and something you will use over and over again.

If you are a product-based business, have quality shots taken on a white background that can be used by the media. Using a white background is standard in the industry, making it easy for you to send an acceptable sample photo of your product to a journalist. They will usually request high-resolution photos they can use rather than having you send the product for photographing.

Should you be caught off guard and quickly need a photograph, learn tips on shooting your own photography from expert photographer, Monica True, in Expert's Corner at www.prforanyone.com/experts-corner.

I didn't know it at the time, but the best money I invested early on was for creating high-quality product shots for my website. I have used these photographs many times for media placements.

The same holds true for a headshot. Find a local photographer who specializes in headshots. Anyone seeking media exposure needs a good headshot. This inexpensive investment will be worth its weight in gold.

EXPERT TIP

If you are going to shoot your own photography, take photographs outside using natural light. You can use things you have at home or in your garage, such as white poster board or a white Styrofoam cooler top, to help reflect the light and avoid shadows.

—**Monica True,** Monica True Photography,
www.monicatrue.com.

Tip # 6
Your Brand Is Your "Buzz"

A brand for a company is like a reputation for a person.
—**Jeff Bezos**

Branding your business is important because it communicates to the world what your business represents and who you are. Basically, your brand is your reputation.

You want your branding to be consistent across everything you do. It starts with your logo and goes from your website, to your blog, to your social media, to your business cards. Everything you submit to the media about your business should be consistent. Use the same logo, the same fonts, and the same marketing messages. Design templates that are all similar, using the same logo placement and color schemes. If you have a tagline, use it in everything.

Every aspect of your business should reinforce the other parts.

MY FAVORITE TIP

When I launched CastMedic Designs, I hired a local graphic artist who worked out of his house with very reasonable rates. He created my business card, letterhead, catalog, and marketing pieces that were all consistent, so I could send out a cohesively branded marketing package.

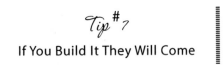

Tip #7
If You Build It They Will Come

Be a yardstick of quality. Some people aren't used to an environment where excellence is expected.

—Steve Jobs

It's time to start building your brand. Maybe you already have a logo, but your message is inconsistent throughout other parts of your business. Maybe you haven't started yet or you've got some things going or you need to start over. You need to get everything working together.

Whatever the case may be, there are several inexpensive online resources to help you with logo design, graphics, and templates.

As I mentioned earlier, use <u>www.fiverr.com</u>, where you can get just about anything done for $5.00, or <u>www.elance.</u>

com, www.odesk.com, and www.99designs.com, where you can submit proposals and have freelancers bid on your jobs.

A great printing resource is Got Print at www.gotprint.com. You can purchase 1,000 business cards for around $40.00 including shipping. I also love the specials you can find at Vista Print, www.vistaprint.com. Sign up for their mailing list as they frequently email percentage off offers.

MY FAVORITE TIP

I used oDesk for the PR for Anyone™ logo and it was only $35.00. When the artist was done I received the logo in jpeg, pdf, and ai formats in both color and black and white. He also did a graphic version (using the black circle) and a print friendly version without the circle. Everything was done in about three days.

Tip #8
Blow Their Minds

Always do right. This will gratify some people, and astonish the rest.

—Mark Twain

It amazes me how many businesses don't understand customer service and how it effects their PR. In today's age of social media and online review sites, why wouldn't you want to provide excellent customer service?

Of my 50,000+ products, occasionally something isn't right. I've had rhinestones fall off or the petals of a daisy come apart. The few times I have received disappointing emails, I replied immediately, told my customer to throw it away, and I sent a replacement out the next day. They are utterly shocked and profusely grateful with my response. Do other businesses really not take care of their clients? Not only can an unhappy customer share their frustration with a potential customer, but a media outlet may also be watching.

Always do the right thing with your customers!

MY FAVORITE TIP

When I owned the retail store, we told our employees we were a "yes" store and to treat our customers as such. We would bend over backwards to keep our customers happy and find anything they needed. We survived owning a high-end retail store in a blighted town, during the economic crash, because of our amazing customer service.

Tip #9
Alert!

Did you know that there are free services that allow you to set alerts online which can help you gain more publicity? These include: Google Alerts at www.google.com/alerts, Mention at en.mention.net, and Talkwalker at www. talkwalker.com/alerts.

These are online clipping services that search the Web to see if you or your business has been mentioned (see next tip for clipping services).

They allow you to monitor anything on the Web, then send you an email as soon as something for which you set an alert appears in their search results.

Everyone should be using one or all of these services to keep track of what is being said about them online. They are easy and free and the results are incredible.

Some basics alerts you should have set up are:

- Your name
- Your business name
- Your business competitors
- The topic of your business
- Your key business words

If you have a common name such as John Smith, you'll need to add another search term that makes it unique, or you'll be receiving thousands of results for every John Smith in the world. Try John Smith and your business name or John Smith and your city.

For my business, if I can get a celebrity to wear my product, it's amazing PR.

One of my most successful Google Alerts has been "celebrity broken foot." The Paparazzi doesn't have anything on Google and me!

This alert has resulted in my finding several celebrities in medical boots to whom I reached out and inspired to make their medical boot fashionable, including: Demi Lovato, Diana Ross, and Olympic Gold Medalist, Jordyn Wieber, as well as several local news anchors and a host from QVC.

Another way to use these alerts is to build relationships with journalists. You can find out who is writing about your expertise. Then reach out to them by commenting on their articles or offering your services for future stories.

If you are an author of a specific topic that a journalist covers, ask them if they would be interested in a copy of your book.

Tip #10
Clip, Clip, Clip

Press clipping services, also known as media monitoring, are a way for businesses to track media coverage and determine what's being said about them and their competitors. It's similar to Google Alerts, Mention, and Talkwalker, but on a grander scale, and includes television, radio, newspapers, magazines, and social media. Google doesn't always index trade publications, small newspapers, or regional online sources, so there is limited information on where and when your company is being mentioned.

While media monitoring services can be more accurate than using Google and the others, they are not free, and can be quite costly depending on the level of service provided.

I recommend starting at these sites to determine if one is right for you:

Burrelles Luce, www.burrellesluce.com
Cision, us.cision.com/media-monitoring/media-monitoring-overview.asp
Vocus, www.vocus.com/advanced-pr/monitor
CyberAlert, www.cyberalert.com
WebClipping, webclipping.com

Different services offer different levels of monitoring, so these are just a few examples of what's available.

Tip #11
Going Up

I'm sure you have heard the expression, "The Elevator Pitch." This narrative is a 30-second sales pitch about you, your company, or your product. You should be able to recite it freely as it could be something you have to do quickly with a journalist or someone interested in your company.

The concept of an elevator pitch is that if you had to tell someone about your company while riding in an elevator, how would you do it in that limited amount of time?

My elevator pitch is:

I'm Christina Daves, Founder of CastMedic Designs. We design and manufacture MediFashions, which are accessories to make walking medical boots fashion-forward, helping the injured look and heal their best and experience The Healing Power of Fashion®.

MY FAVORITE TIP
Liken your elevator pitch to a tweet. Get your message across briefly and to the point in 140 characters or less.

Tip #12
Knowledge Is Power

Try, try, try, and keep on trying is the rule that must be followed to become an expert in anything.

—W. Clement Stone

If you want to be *the* expert who is quoted on your topic, you should be able to talk about it effortlessly. Even if you think you know everything there is to know, learn more. In this book I share my personal experiences, but I also went out and interviewed experts to make sure you could hear from them as well. Become the most knowledgeable person on your topic, present it well, and the media will come to you.

Tip # 13
Just Be Yourself

The authentic self is the soul made visible.

—Sarah Ban Breathnach

Nobody likes a phony. People want authenticity. When you are seeking PR or being interviewed, remember to stay true to yourself and your brand. Don't try to be something you're not. Being genuine and authentic will pay off in spades and should result in more interviews and more media coverage.

When I interviewed Natalie Mashaal, who got her producing start on the *Oprah Winfrey Show*, I specifically asked her how people such as, Dr. Oz, Dr. Phil, and Suze Orman became Oprah's go-to experts. She said it was their authenticity. They were real and believable, and the audience could relate to them. You can listen to her interview in Expert's Corner, www.prforanyone.com/experts-corner.

IT'S A WRAP

No matter what happens, always be yourself.
—Dale Carnegie

In this section you learned that PR involves a great deal more than sending a press release (which we'll cover later in the book). While press releases are important, don't forget that it's your presence, your personality, and your overall brand that is the cornerstone of your PR efforts. Look professional, be consistent in your message, and be authentic and you'll be on your way to success!

Shout It From the Rooftops

In life you are either the passenger or a pilot, it's your choice.

—Anonymous

If you want to gain media exposure, you're going to have to do some work and put yourself out there. It's unlikely the media is going to come banging on your door just because you've hung an "Open for Business" sign.

This section provides you with ways to gain exposure for your business, leads you to new potential customers, and possibly helps you score a little local media coverage.

Tip #14
Get Up And Talk

If you are comfortable with it, and not everyone is, a great way to gain exposure is to speak. Come up with a topic or workshop idea, then sign up with local chambers of commerce and business networking groups. Speaking is a great way to gain exposure to potential customers. Often, there are members of the press covering these events, so there is the potential for them to cover your business too.

I was asked to speak at a women's forum for our local chamber of commerce, and a few days later my name popped up in Google Alerts. A newspaper reporter wrote about the event and used a photograph of me speaking, along with my name and company name in the photo caption of the article.

As you continue to speak and gain experience and credibility, you should be able to apply for speaking at larger, national events, and of course there is more opportunity for national media exposure in that arena.

Both Toastmasters, www.toastmasters.org and National Speakers Association, www.nsaspeaker.org are organizations to assist you with public speaking engagements.

Tip #15
Radio-Active

Practice Makes Perfect

—Unknown

When trying to gain media exposure, everyone wants to start with the golden crown of morning television, such as the *Today Show* or *Good Morning America*. It is, however, very unlikely for you to start on a show such as this. You first need to earn your wings and establish yourself as an expert. If it makes you feel any better, I have an acquaintance in one of my networking groups who tried for ten years to get on the *Today Show,* and she finally landed a spot this year. (We'll discuss perseverance later in the book.)

If you are nervous right now just thinking about getting media exposure, imagine if your very first experience was on a nationally broadcast live morning show? If you bomb, that's it! There probably won't be a next time.

I'm not trying to scare you. I just want you to have realistic PR aspirations as a newbie. Remember, I landed everything I did in one year, so it doesn't have to take a long time. It's just important to get a few interviews under your belt first.

How do you gain experience?

Blog Talk Radio has over 25,000 monthly shows and almost 8 million listeners. This medium is a great place to start and become comfortable with being interviewed.

Submit a Google search on your topic. For example, I might Google, "inventor interviews" or "mompreneuer interviews" and approach them with a great idea for an interview. (We'll get to that soon.)

I was very nervous on my first radio interview. I think I did okay, but if anyone would have had a stethoscope on my chest, it would have broken their eardrums. Since that first interview, I've done dozens more. I love doing radio and have become pretty good at it. Now I feel much more comfortable approaching nationally syndicated shows because I have experience.

The same holds true for webcasts or podcasts. When you participate in these interviews, not only is it great experience, you are establishing a presence on the Internet adding to your search engine optimization (SEO*) which, in turn, drives customers to your website.

Before approaching someone for a potential interview, determine how strong their website is. Go to www.alexa.com and enter their domain name. Websites are ranked based on how they compare to all other relative sites on the web over the past three months. The site with the highest combination of unique visitors and page views is ranked #1, which happens to be Google.

Make sure the potential interviewer's site has some type of ranking to make it worth your while to hold the interview.

MY FAVORITE TIP

Always be prepared for an interview. Ask the host if they would prefer sample questions you generate ahead of time or if they are going to send you their planned questions. Provide a bio. Send them your headshot for their website and promotion of the show. Make sure you know how long your interview will be and be ready to speak for that amount of time. Don't sell. The host won't forget why you are there, and you'll be able to talk about your business. Remember, you are there to provide content to their audience.

*SIDENOTE: I hope everyone reading this book is aware of search engine optimization (SEO) and is using that on their

website and blog. I am by no means an expert in SEO and am not providing anything other than basic information on this topic.

It is vital for you as a business owner to know what the keywords applicable to your business are and to use them in anything you do online. Using effective keywords on your site means you come up earlier in Google rankings when someone searches for that keyword. This process is also known as "organic search rankings" should you want to research the topic on your own. Google is constantly changing the way they handle SEO and keywords, so do your homework.

Tip # 16

Be a Gracious Guest

Either write something worth reading or do something worth writing.

—Benjamin Franklin

I was not a writer, but I had to learn. The Internet is full of content and people looking to fill their pages. I have been asked repeatedly to guest blog, write articles, and offer content for other sites. Though it's been difficult for me to turn myself into a writer, it has been invaluable for creating links back to my website which helps with search engine optimization (SEO) and generating new leads for my business. It is also establishing me as an expert in my industry.

Use Google and research the top blogs in your industry. Before you approach someone about guest blogging for them, find out what they've already published on their site and determine where you can fill in any voids on existing topics.

MY FAVORITE TIP

Remember when guest writing, make sure you use your top SEO terms, so that when the article is published it will link back to your site.

Tip[#] *17*
The Giving Tree

No one has ever become poor by giving.

—Anne Frank

Linking your business to a charity or worthy cause is always a great way to generate publicity. Not only are you helping a cause you believe in, but hosting a charity event, donating a portion of the proceeds of sales, or donating product or services to a charity can be a positive PR coup as well. It puts you in a good light in the eyes of your customers, and there is always the possibility of media coverage.

I am a firm believer in giving back. Please don't give to charity just to try to gain publicity. In the long run, the good deed will do more for your PR than any media exposure you might get out of it, and you will feel good about giving back.

EXPERT TIP

According to a recent survey by Nielsen, half of global consumers are willing to pay more for goods and services from a company that gives back to society.

Tip # *18*

And The Winner Is . . .

Do not wait to strike till the iron is hot; but make it hot by striking.

—**William B. Sprague**

Look for awards and contests for which you can apply. Participating in and winning anything is a great opportunity for PR. There are tons of contests for new businesses, new products, websites, social media influencers, "Best Of's," just about anything you can imagine. And with the Internet, they are easy to find. Don't forget to search locally too. Winning a local award is great for more local exposure.

Check your local chambers of commerce, local and national business groups, and local and national publications for any awards they host. Google is a great resource to find awards. Even if you see a contest or award that has been given already, set it in your online alerts, and you'll be notified when it opens for the following year.

My first year in business, I was named one of the "Top 200 Leading Moms in Business" by StartupNation. I didn't win, but I was recognized, and I still use that designation today in my email signature.

I also applied for "WomenInventorz Network Woman Inventor of the Year for 2013" and was named a finalist.

MY FAVORITE TIP
One of my Google Alerts is set for "product contest," another for "business award." This way, I receive

notifications when pertinent contests or awards are announced.

Tip #19
The Award Goes To

Not only can you apply for an award, you can also create an award or scholarship that your company can hand out every year. It can be a small scholarship for a student-athlete or an award to a person in your community making a difference. You should be able to generate local buzz for giving this type of award. Even though it will be the recipient who is covered, you will gain peripheral media coverage as well.

Tip #20
Host a Shin-Dig

Can you launch your business or product with an event and invite the media to attend? Keep in mind that an event could end up being quite costly, so there are probably much better ways to invest your start-up funds. If, however, you have the contacts or can work with someone in a collaborative effort, a unique event could be a way to gain exposure. Don't forget to invite the media using the tools we'll discuss later in the book.

MY FAVORITE TIP
When we opened Details for the Home, we worked with our town Mayor's office to host a ribbon-cutting ceremony.

They invited other local dignitaries and notified the press, and we were covered in all of our local newspapers.

Tip #21
Get a Free Ride

Talk to your local university and see if there is an undergraduate or graduate public relations course and if they would be willing to use your business as a class or individual project.

I submitted CastMedic Designs as a potential project for graduate students at Trinity University in Washington, D.C. We were chosen, and one of the students prepared a wonderful campaign that involved Children's Hospital that I am working to implement. It was something which I hadn't thought of and full of great ideas. Personally, I love working with both high school and college students because they have such fresh, creative minds, and are so eager to learn and impress.

Your Message In a Bottle

ou've got something really important and newsworthy to share with the world, whether it's about you, your company or something you've done. How do you share the news?

First and foremost, let me re-emphasize *newsworthy*. Sending out a press release just to say, "Hey I'm great! Buy my stuff!" is not what the media wants to see. Journalists are looking for story ideas their audience is going to *want* to learn about. Imagine yourself sitting on your front porch with a cup of coffee, reading the newspaper or a magazine. What is it that you would want to read about?

Some newsworthy topics could include:

- Landing a major contract or client
- Launching a new product

- Announcing a contest
- Receiving or giving an award
- Significant donation to a charity
- A grand opening
- Fundraisers
- Hiring a key executive

Before you send anything out, ask yourself if you would be interested in hearing the story or learning more about the topic. If your answer is yes, read on to learn various methods for sharing your story.

Tip #*22*

Tell The World You're Here!

New is what all journalists are looking for. They want the "scoop." They want to be the first to report on a new idea, new product, or new business. As busy as you might be right when you launch your business, don't forget to send out an initial announcement in a press release, telling the world you are here. It is likely that you will gain some sort of media coverage just from announcing something new.

Don't worry if you aren't "new" anymore. Reinvent yourself by creating something new about your company. Do you have a new product? A big new client? Can you collaborate with someone on a new concept? Think creatively about how you can reinvent yourself or your business and create something new that can become newsworthy.

Tip # 23

For Immediate Release

The press is the best instrument for enlightening the mind of man, and improving him as a rational, moral, and social being.

—Thomas Jefferson

Now for a quick history of the press release (because I think it's a pretty cool story).

It all started back in 1954 when PRNewswire created an electronic system for distributing press releases. Before that, a release was sent either by messenger or mail. Just imagine how long it would take your story to get to press back then! In 1972, PRNewswire was sold to Western Union, who had all of the telecommunications lines in place for electronic transmission and became what is now the modern day wire service.

Today, with the ability to make a direct connection with just about anyone via email and social media, the days of writing a press release, sending it out, and automatically getting vast coverage are pretty much gone. You might gain some exposure if you have something really great to share such as starting a unique company or launching a new product concept. And, you could get really lucky on a slow news day.

The press release, however, is not dead and still serves very important functions in PR:

- It allows you to share your message with a large audience.
- It drives traffic to your website, which can increase sales.
- It enhances credibility.
- It increases your visibility in search engines.

Whenever writing a press release, make sure your business' keywords are located in the first 100 words of the press release to assist in search engine optimization (SEO). If including links in your release back to your website, make sure the first link is optimized to your keywords on that page of your website. If this concept sounds like a foreign language to you, I recommend looking into keyword optimization and search engine optimization.

When you mass distribute a press release, which we will discuss later in this section, Google will begin to classify you or your business under your keywords. No single press release will jump you to page one of Google. But it will increase your Google credibility and establish your brand online.

So what exactly is a press release?

It is the who, what, when, where, and why of your company, product, story, or event. It's really that simple. There is a standard format for a press release that includes the following components:

- Contact Information—whom should the media contact? [name, phone, email, and website—include your logo]. This information should be located right at the top and easy to see.

- FOR IMMEDIATE RELEASE or FOR RELEASE ON [date] goes on the top of the press release. Do you want your release to go out ASAP or should it be held until a certain date?

- Use a great headline! Peak the reader's curiosity about what's in the release based on the title, AKA "The Hook." The title should be bold and centered on the top and no more than 60 characters.

Here are some helpful headline ideas:

- ◊ Tie in a trend.
- ◊ Create controversy.
- ◊ Provide tips.
- ◊ Associate with current events.
- ◊ Apply seasonality.
- ◊ Use celebrity.

- A subhead is located immediately below the headline and gives a bit more description about the headline. It is also intended to pique additional interest to engage the reader.

- City, State, and Date—At the beginning of the first paragraph.

- Body—300-500 words. Hyperlink back to your website. Add images and videos.
  - ◊ Paragraph #1—Contains the lead or the first 100 words. These are the most important words and should tell the who, what, why, when, and where. Entice the reader to want more. But

give enough information so that it can stand on its own.

◊ Paragraphs #2 & 3—Contain supporting information, statistics, quotes. Make key points stand out.

◊ Paragraphs #4 & 5—Contain the least critical information, a summary of what you've written about or supporting information. Odds are, nobody will read this far into the release.

Company/Organization Boilerplate—Standard information about your company. This section is the same on every release. It's just a short company bio.

Three hashtags together indicate that your press release is complete and the reader knows there is no additional information. These are located at the bottom, centered on the page.

Always try to keep press releases to one page. To see sample press releases visit:

service.prweb.com/who-uses-it/examples-by-industry
www.ereleases.com/i/BigPressReleaseBook.pdf

When writing a press release, think as a reporter would and create a newsworthy story that creates value for the media and one that many people would want to read. Create a story angle from the journalist's perspective, not a business owner's. Ask yourself, *Would I want to hear this story?*

This is the first press release I ever sent out, and the company got quite a bit of coverage as a result, even sparking several spin-off articles. Not bad for a beginner!

CASTMEDIC
DESIGNS

Contact: Christina Daves
(xxx) xxx-xxxx
christina@castmedicdesigns.com
www.castmedicdesigns.com

FOR IMMEDIATE RELEASE

WARNING: With This Product, You May WANT to Break a Leg!

CastMedic Designs Invites you to Experience... *The Healing Power of Fashion*®

GAINESVILLE, VA - CastMedic Designs wants people who suffer an injury to experience the "Healing Power of Fashion" with an exciting, innovative new line of MediFashions™ - fashion accessories for medical walking boots. This first of its kind product is revolutionizing the medical industry by showing consumers that adding fashion to function when placed in bulky, unattractive medical devices brings a positive experience to the healing process. Studies show that an optimistic outlook helps in the recovery process and CastMedic Designs offers people the opportunity to Look and Heal Their Best!

This unique line of accessories provides the opportunity for both adults and children to accessorize medical boots for school, work, or play and allows people the chance to have some fun while recovering from an injury, instead of being self conscious about it.   People are going to stare at the boot anyway, now they'll say, "Oh my gosh! That is so cute!"

It all began in the Summer of 2010 when Christina Daves, founder of CastMedic Designs, broke her foot and was placed in a walking medical boot for eight weeks. She scoured the Internet for anything to "dress-up" her boot but unfortunately, nothing of its kind existed. She also noticed that when celebrities like Reese Witherspoon and Halle Berry were recently in boots, they had nothing to help them look stylish. In fact, Halle Berry skipped the 2012 Oscars because she was in a boot.

Seeing a need in the marketplace, the former retail store owner started designing and coming up with products that were both fashionable and fun to use to accessorize the boots. Her feeling was, *"with at least 1.5 to 2.5 million walking medical boots prescribed annually, why should that many people have to walk around in a big ugly boot? Why not have some fun?* " (figures based on 2008 Medicare statistics and data complied from orthopedic surgeons and podiatrists)

Products include:
*   Wrap-Its - decorative faux fur cuffs to wrap around the top of the boot
*   Stap-Its - flowers and faux fur accessories that are attached on any strap of the boot
*   Click-Its - a children's line of pin back buttons worn on any strap of the boot
*   Sock-Its - decorative "socks" worn over the liner of the boot

With close to 60 products to choose from including faux-fur wraps, decorative "socks", flowers, and themed buttons for children, there is no reason anyone has to be unhappy in a boot ever again. We all know the old adage, "laughter is the best medicine" but in fact this is a true statement.

CastMedic Designs was created to bring fashion and fun to the medical industry beginning with walking medical boots. It is their mission to bring "The Healing Power of Fashion"® to a mainly function-only industry and provide consumers an opportunity to feel good about themselves while healing from an injury.

###

The Healing Power of Fashion®

Tip # 24
The Art of the Hook

Think left and think right and think low and think high. Oh, the thinks you can think up if only you try.

—Dr. Seuss

The first thing anyone sees when looking at a press release is the heading. Whether they like it or not will determine whether they go any further in reading your release. It is vital to create a catchy heading that will stand out.

You won't get a second chance to make this first impression.

We didn't title our press release: "CastMedic Designs Launches New Product." Instead, we used the word WARNING in all caps, implying how people would *want* to break a leg for this product. This heading made it intriguing. People wanted to find out what product would make someone *want* to break their leg?

Here are some suggestions based on our headline ideas above:

- Tie in a trend—*US Weekly Magazine* recently ran a segment dear to my heart about celebrities decorating their medical devices entitled:
  "Pimp My Injury!" *For these hurting stars, a little bling can ease the pain.*
- Create controversy—Steve Olsher, www.steveolsher.com, used this hook to land a segment on *FOX* television in Chicago:
  "College is the Single Worst Investment a Parent Can Make for their Child"
- Provide tips—Read any national magazine, and you'll see articles based on tips. This heading is from a recent issue of *Real Simple* magazine:
  "6 Items to Simplify Your Life"
- Associate with current events—This sample hook was in *e-Releases Big Press Release Book*:

"Growing Up Is Never Easy: The Pains of Recession Should Lead to More Mature Financial Practices"

- Apply seasonality—Jennifer Fugo of Gluten Free School, www.glutenfreeschool.com, recently used this hook discussing gluten:

  "What You Don't Know is Hiding on Your Grill Can Make You Sick This July 4th"

- Use celebrity—I share this story later in the book and you can hear him tell it at www.prforanyone.com/experts-corner, but an acquaintance of mine, Rich Moore, got quite a bit of coverage—and a little surprise with:

  "What I Learned from Donald Trump"

Tip # 25
Going Viral

If a picture is worth a thousand words, then a video is priceless.

—Anonymous

When I shot my first video, it was truly awful! I had to submit a video with a funding application, so I sat in front of my laptop, taped sticky notes all around the screen, and tried to look and sound comfortable. It was so bad it's no wonder I never heard back from anyone!

That was literally a year ago. Now, I'm going all over the country interviewing really important people for Expert's Corner, and I absolutely love being on camera. I keep that original video on my computer to remind myself of how easy it is to conquer obstacles and improve.

Video is the wave of the future, and the online news release services make it very easy to embed videos in a press release. How often have you heard of a video that "went viral"? Posting a video online allows people to share it on their social networks and gives the news media and bloggers something to repost and/or use.

As with keywords mentioned previously, video is a great way to assist in search engine optimization (SEO) by using keywords in the title and tagging those words when you upload the video to a free hosting service such as YouTube or Vimeo. If the video is repeatedly shared on other sites, it continues to build links to your website and assists in strengthening your SEO.

If you find you are uncomfortable in front of the camera, just keep practicing. You will get better and better at it.

MY FAVORITE TIP

There is the greatest app called Telemprompt+ that lets you convert your iPad into a teleprompter. It's $14.99 and can be found on iTunes. Type in your script, set the speed, and you're all set. This App has saved me on many occasions.

Tip #*26*
Pitch Perfect

Don't forget to proofread, proofread, proofread. These are after all, journalists. Make sure the entire press release is free from grammatical and typographical errors and that all links work correctly. Double-check statistics and facts. In some instances, a journalist might just print your entire press release, or portions thereof, so it is critical that what you send out is perfect.

Tip #27
You Get What You Pay For

Now that your press release is written, you need to find a press release distribution service. As with the media query services, there are free and paid distribution services.

The paid services come with bells and whistles, and as I'm sure you can guess, if you pay to have your press release distributed, it will get to more outlets. I recommend using the paid release on your initial launch or if you have significant and/or breaking news information to share.

Here are some options of available paid services:

- PRNewswire—This is the original press release service, www.prnewswire.com.
- eReleases—I used eReleases on the first press release I distributed because I got a great deal as a first time customer. I was on a tight budget and didn't have many options. I got quite a bit of traction from that initial release, www.ereleases.com.
- PRWeb—I have also used PRWeb with great success, www.prweb.com.

The bottom line is that any of these services are going over the major news wire services, so you really can't go wrong with any of them. Assess your budget, search for a good deal, and send that first release out.

Depending on your financial situation and the news you have to share, you might want to continue to send press releases out over these sites. I choose to do this sparingly and instead, submit press release/story ideas to specific journalists at specific publications. This system is discussed in detail later in this chapter.

When writing a press release, always think about search engine optimization (SEO). Make sure your key search terms are located early in the release. If you aren't sure what your terms should be, it might be worth hiring an expert to figure these out for you.

MY FAVORITE TIP

I'll share a little trick I learned about the paid news release sites. Register on all of them, and you will likely be sent a first-time user coupon code or discount. I sent two releases out (using two different companies) during the first eight months I was in business. Each cost about $250, which I thought was pretty reasonable to gain some national attention. I used the paid services for the launch of the company, and again when I won the inventor's competition on the *Steve Harvey Show*. Both received quite a bit of coverage.

Tip #28
Spread the Word

If you are just submitting a routine press release about something newsworthy that you aren't sending to a particular journalist and likely won't catch the eye of the major national media, you might want to consider using a free service. This service still gets the release out and seen, and also continues to build search engine optimization (SEO).

As I mentioned earlier, the press release is an important component in PR, specifically for SEO. There are several free distribution services that assist in gaining exposure for the press release as well as building credibility and SEO for your business:

- www.prlog.org
- www.free-press-release.com
- www.onlineprnews.com
- www.newswiretoday.com
- www.openpr.com

Remember, even though these services are free, you only want to release content that is newsworthy.

Tip #29
Online Buzz

Using social media is vital to generate buzz for your company. It is the easiest way to spread your message to a large audience. Most of the distribution services will offer an automatic announcement feature for Twitter and Facebook. Don't forget to share your press release on your own social media sites as well. If the release is very topic specific and you follow a journalist on Twitter or Facebook and think they would be interested in the story, send it to them personally. That usually works best if you have already established some type of relationship with the journalist.

Tip #30
Who Cares?

Who is your target audience? Who would want to know about your newsworthy story?

Start building a list of specific media outlets such as television shows, news programs, radio shows, magazines, newspapers, and blogs that report on similar topics. These contacts are the ones you will approach with a targeted story idea. Instead of sending a blanket press release, you will target specific writers, producers, and bloggers with a very targeted story idea in hopes that they will cover it.

Tip #31
On Target

A targeted story idea is one that is personalized for the format of a television or radio show, or a magazine. It is very important to know the show or publication before you send a targeted story idea. You wouldn't want to send a story about crowdfunding to *Parents Magazine*.

The media is always looking for fresh ideas, so if you've got something, send it in. I recommend doing it via email as that seems to be the preferred medium of journalists.

Remember that the media are inundated with email, so yours needs to stand out. I heard a *CNBC* journalist say he receives anywhere from 500 to 1,000 emails per day. Don't send a lengthy email. Make it easy for them.

This is the formula we use that works well:

Segment Idea: Catchy Title—See TIP #24—The Art of the Hook

Talking Points: Provide a bulleted list of 3-5 talking points (add a statistic or quote if relevant)

Visuals: Media loves visuals

Experience: Mention if you have media experience and put a link to a press kit or website showing prior media experience

Photos: Head Shot/Product Shot/Book Cover

Contact Information: Name, email, and phone number

Tip #32
Keep It On The "Down Low"

Visuals are a critical component in today's quest for media. Always send low-resolution photos, but let the media know that high-resolution photos are available. You don't want to clog up or delay their email inbox with huge image files.

Tip #33

A Present? For Me?

If you think you would be better served having a reporter or editor touch and feel your product or learn about your business first-hand, you could opt to send the traditional press kit. A press kit contains your press release, bio, photos, and samples.

Whatever you're sending, whether an envelope or a package, make yourself stand out. Use bright colored envelopes and folders. Use big type on the envelope. If you are sending product, be creative.

I learned this lesson the hard way. I went to New York City with a friend and designated one day out of our trip to be my big PR campaign stop. I made about fifteen packets in manila folders and headed to the main offices of all the major magazines on Avenue of the Americas. I walked into the main lobby, fully confident, went right up to the receptionist and said, "I have a package to drop off for Ms. Editor of *Fashion Magazine.*"

They directed me to the mailroom, which is a room located outside the building around the corner of the main building. I walked in, and I am not kidding when I tell you that the entire mail reception desk was five deep with beautiful colorful bags with silk ribbons and gorgeous wrapped boxes and branded packages with tulle and balloons. My heart sank as I looked down at my manila envelopes. I left them, but realized that they might not even get past the mail clerk downstairs, who would probably pick and deliver all the pretty packages first. Not surprisingly, I didn't hear back from anyone after those deliveries.

Be unique. Be different. As I continue to say, think outside the box. One thing that continues to get me noticed is the delicious custom cookies I have made by a local specialty baker. They are designed as medical boots decorated in a leopard Sock-It, one of my products. on.fb.me/16IfzmR.

Tip #*34*
Join Forces

No person will make a great business who wants to do it all himself or get all the credit.

—Andrew Carnegie

Come up with a good way to present your ideas, especially if you are a product-based business. Products are difficult to place by themselves and most magazines won't write about one specific product. You will stand a much better chance of placing your story if it relates to a bigger picture theme or topic.

Don't be afraid to collaborate with other people. My product helps people feel better about themselves when they're injured. I reached out to a handful of other product-based entrepreneurs with similar concepts to see if they would be interested in collaborating on a segment entitled: *Healing in Style*. Then, I found a doctor with extensive media experience and asked if she would be the expert to speak to the positive psychology of feeling better about yourself when you look better. We just recently started sending this story concept out to the media and are looking forward to great results.

We Want YOU!

Your uniqueness is your greatest strength, not how well you emulate others.

—Simon S. Tam

When the judge said, "*We pick* (long, dramatic pause…) *The Boot!*"

I was stunned! Did she really say that? "The Boot!" That was me—I had the boot. It meant they had picked me. I won!

At that moment I knew exactly how Miss America or an Academy Award® winner feels when they say, "*I'm shocked! I really didn't expect to win.*"

Nobody plopped a giant tiara on my head or handed me a golden statue. Even better, I had just won $20,000 on the

Steve Harvey Show's Inventor Competition for my medical boot fashion accessories!

This moment of greatness stemmed from the three minutes it took me to respond to a producer's query.

You don't think it's that easy to gain media coverage? Think again, because it really is.

Reporters are looking for people like you to help them with their stories. They need sources and experts they can quote. Television and radio shows need guests every single day. And bloggers are always on the hunt for new information.

You can become an expert in the media for free. All you have to do is sign up for media query services. They will send you daily emails from journalists about the topics being covered.

Respond regularly to these queries with good content and you will start to see consistent media coverage, while you build valuable relationships. It's really that easy.

Remember, it takes time. If you don't hear back right away, be patient. Continue to respond in a timely manner and always be on-topic. Allow time for the journalists to recognize your expertise and to start using you in stories. I had answered the query for the *Steve Harvey Show* in August. By the time I heard back in October, I had almost completely forgotten about it.

Tip #*35*

Free Press #1 – Help a Reporter Out/HARO

My favorite free service is Help a Reporter Out (HARO). Their website is www.helpareporterout.com, and all you have to do is visit the site, sign up and—voila!—media queries will start appearing in your mailbox that day.

The basic service is completely free and is comprised of journalists looking for experts or people who can comment on topics about which they are writing.

During the week, three times a day (at around 6:00 a.m., 12:00 p.m., and 6:00 p.m., EST, excluding holidays) you will receive email queries from reporters, authors, and bloggers who are looking for experts, quotes, and information on stories they are writing. You will even see queries from television producers looking for guests.

There are between twenty and forty queries each time and rarely is there a duplicate query throughout the day.

Hands down, I have had the most success with HARO.

In fact, I am listed as one of their top success stories because of the *Steve Harvey Show*. I answered a query that simply said: *Do you have a product you want to take to the next level? (National Television).*

My response led to a reply email several months later, a series of interviews, and ultimately an appearance on the *Steve Harvey Show* as a contestant for their inventor's competition. That little query changed my life. Of course, I had to sell the show on my product and on myself after I was initially selected. But it was HARO that opened the door.

What I love about HARO, and have truly embraced, is their tagline, "Everyone's an Expert at Something." I was fortunate to be able to interview Peter Shankman, who founded HARO, for Expert's Corner. You can hear his interview at www.prforanyone.com/experts-corner. He is the one who initially started me thinking about responding to media queries and about what I could share.

Before starting with HARO, ask yourself what expertise you plan on sharing with the world.

I found, based on my experiences, I could respond to queries related to the following and have been quoted as an expert for many articles on these topics:

- Start-ups
- Entrepreneurship
- Mompreneurs
- Invention
- Manufacturing
- Wholesale
- Retail
- Patent/trademark
- Publicity
- General business
- Women-owned business
- Brick and mortar retail store
- Service-based industry
- E-commerce
- Business financing
- Motherhood
- Parenting
- and more…

I created a product from an idea and brought it to market. I also owned three businesses prior to launching CastMedic Designs. And, I'm the mother of two very pleasant teenagers. That in itself makes me a parenting expert. Because of this experience, I am knowledgeable and have expertise in all of these areas. Don't sell your knowledge or expertise short.

The ideas above should help you get your creative juices flowing. Make a list of your areas of expertise, and use your list as a guide when responding to queries.

EXPERT TIP

Professionalism is the #1 tip for pitching reporters on HARO. This tip may sound obvious, but we often hear from reporters that the pitches they receive are poorly written. A well-crafted pitch is free of slang, spelling mistakes, and grammatical errors. This shows the reporter that you mean business. Don't sacrifice quality and professionalism in order to respond quickly. Put your best foot forward and you'll immediately increase your chances of success.

—**Natalia Dykyj,** Director, Product Management, Vocus (HARO's parent company)

Tip #*36*
Free Press #2 – Profnet Connect

ProfNet Connect is affiliated with PR Newswire, the oldest news wire service in the country. Their free media query service is called ProfNet Connect. Anyone can access their site, fill out a profile, and be listed as an expert. Journalists search the database, and if they see a fit, will contact you directly.

ProfNet describes their network as "an online, social-media component that allows someone to easily connect with journalists, bloggers, and other communication professionals."

This service is different from the other media query services because there is nothing proactive you can do in terms of responding to a query and starting to build a relationship with journalists. The journalists find you based on your submitted profile.

Sign up for free at www.profnetconnect.com.

$\mathcal{T}\!ip$ #*37*
Free Press #3 – Pitchrate.com

What I like about PitchRate is that you can insert a photo with a bio that is attached to every query response you submit. They also offer to upload your press kit with their paid service, Online Press Kit 24/7, and include that with your query responses. There is a monthly fee to attach a press kit, so I opted to respond to just the free queries.

According to their founding company, Wasabi Communications, "PitchRate.com is a free media matchmaking service providing a powerful tool for journalists looking for sources, and giving experts media coverage opportunities."

Below is a list they put together for us to highlight the benefits of their service:

EXPERT BENEFITS:

- Free media leads, delivered to your email inbox daily.
- PitchRate lets you create a profile that will be attached to every pitch, so you can save time.
- Don't want to read through a whole list of media requests? Designate your expertise choices or search by category or keyword.

- Want to provide even more background information inside your pitch? Attach your online press kit to your profile so journalists can easily link to it.
- Can't remember who you pitched to in the past? Review your pitch history, and keep your inbox tidy by viewing all your media requests online.
- Tired of receiving daily emails? Permanently turn off your daily request feed and view the requests online, or just temporarily stop them while you're on vacation.
- Are you a Publicist? PitchRate lets you create a profile for each of your clients that will be attached to every pitch you make on their behalf.

Sign up for free at www.pitchrate.com.

EXPERT TIP

If you see a media request that speaks to you, don't wait. Make a pitch right away! Once a journalist gets what they need, they may "turn off" their request even if the deadline hasn't been reached. And remember, only respond to requests you can speak about. Irrelevant pitches are considered noise by journalists. Keep your pitches short, simple and concise.

—**Hannah Colson**, Wasabi Publicity (Pitch Rate)

Tip #38

Free Press #4 – Media Diplomat

Media Diplomat is another free reporter query service. This service is unique in that it helps reporters who are writing articles that utilize sources from around the world. The other services mentioned in this section are mainly in North America. Media Diplomat helps connect reporters and experts in Europe, Asia, and Latin America. This service is great for people who are experts on various international topics or can speak specifically on issues in other countries.

Sign up for free at <u>www.mediadiplomat.com</u>.

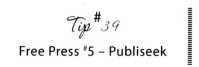

Tip #39
Free Press #5 – Publiseek

Publiseek is, "a free online service that helps storytellers and influencers create better content by connecting them with people, organizations, and brands with great stories to tell." After you sign up, you will receive a daily email with a handful of queries that journalists are working on. If you can speak to that topic, respond to the email.

Sign up for free at: <u>www.publiseek.com.</u>

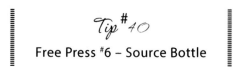

Tip #40
Free Press #6 – Source Bottle

Source Bottle is located in Australia and according to their website, "has journalists from the United States, Canada, UK and Ireland, and New Zealand" as well. Their service is free. Or for $7.95 a month you can add a profile that is submitted with your responses.

As with the other services, you receive an email with various media queries. Within one week of signing up, I had three media "hits" from Source Bottle, one of which was a national publication.

Sign up for free at: www.sourcebottle.com.

Tip #41
Don't Be Late

The early bird gets the worm.

—Norman Ralph Augustine

When you find a query that piques your interest, one of the most important ways of attracting attention is to be timely in your response. HARO, for example, has a huge database, so a reporter may receive hundreds of responses to one query. If the reporter gets a good response right away, anything that comes in afterwards might be disregarded. The best thing you can do is to respond to a pertinent query as soon as possible.

Tip #42
Don't Go "Fishing"

One of the most sincere forms of respect is actually listening to what another has to say.

—Bryant McGill

Do not respond off-topic. Even if the media outlet making the request is one you have been trying to reach through other avenues. Yes, the email will get to them, but they will not be happy that your email has nothing to do with what they are working on at that moment. These journalists are usually up against fast approaching deadlines, so it is a waste of their resources to read responses not pertinent to their query.

With HARO, responding with unrelated information is, in fact, against their policies, and you could be banned from the site if you violate this policy.

MY FAVORITE TIP
Be respectful of the reporter's time!

Tip # *43*
K.I.S.S

Simplicity is the glory of expression.

—Walt Whitman

Reporters don't have time to read lengthy emails. Make your response easy to scan and read. Use bullets if possible and bold important words. Be brief. Some of my biggest successes have come from two-sentence responses.

Provide your contact info. They will get back to you if there is a fit. And I stress this point, do not forget to provide your contact information.

In an interview I conducted with a product manager of HARO, she said I would be shocked at how many people forget to include any contact information. If journalists don't know who you are, they can't contact you.

Lastly, remember how many responses these journalists receive, and don't get frustrated if you don't hear back.

They could have opened one email and found that source to be perfect. The story could have gotten shelved. Or, for example, in the case of my appearance on the *Steve Harvey Show*, I responded to that query in August and didn't hear back for over a month.

Responding to the queries is something you have to commit to diligently. If you do, you will get results.

MY FAVORITE TIP

One of the things I hear over and over is, "I don't have time to answer these queries!" A time-saving tip that I use, is to save specific boilerplate responses I can use for various topics. Because they are already written out and need just a little modification, I can whip up a response to a query in no time. I have sample response emails for queries related to product pitches, business expert, "Mompreneur," start-ups, radio guest, television guest, etc., that require only minor edits. This system allows me to quickly respond to queries on various topics.

Tip # 44
Play Nice

No act of kindness, no matter how small, is ever wasted.
—**Aesop**

If possible, always personalize your queries. Most journalists' names will appear in the query. Go the extra step to address your response directly to the journalist with "Dear (Name)."

Tip #45
No Photos Please

Do not include images with HARO. Their response system strips images. When you respond to a HARO query and want to include an image, you will have to do that via a link to your website. Queries will often ask for images, but you still have to link versus inserting an image. Some queries looking for images will include a personal email address versus the query address. In that case you may respond to their personal email address and attach images.

Tip #46
A Little Birdie Told Me

Twitter is also a great place to find journalists who use the query services. If you see something pertinent, tweet at the journalist. With only 140 characters, your reply needs to be focused and clear. It's great practice to respond to these types of queries.

- Follow HARO at @helpareporter, twitter.com/helpareporter. HARO posts many of their queries on Twitter and they also provide great tips for accessing journalists and how to respond properly.

- If you see #UrgHARO in the tweet, it means a journalist is urgently seeking a source. I often do a quick #UrgHARO search to see if there is anything to which I can respond.
- Follow ProfNet at @ProfNet, <u>twitter.com/ProfNet</u>, where they post press leads all day with deadlines.
- Follow PitchRate at @PitchRate, <u>twitter.com/ pitchrate</u>. They have several urgent queries throughout the day and also provide various tips.
- Follow MediaDiplomat at @MediaDiplomat, <u>twitter. com/mediadiplomat</u>. They do quite a bit of re-tweeting journalists' requests from around Twitter.
- Follow Publiseek at @Publiseek, <u>twitter.com/ Publiseek</u>, where they post various PR updates.
- Follow SourceBottle at @SourceBottle, <u>twitter.com/ sourcebottle</u>. Their Twitter feed is full of media requests.

Another little trick is to search "#journorequest" on Twitter to see what journalists are looking for.

Lastly, www.experttweet.com is a listing of journalists looking for experts. You can go directly to this site, or you can search "#expert" in Twitter to see if any pertinent requests are there.

Tip #47
"Like" Them

The same holds true for Facebook. All of these query services post throughout the day on their Facebook pages. You can find them all at:

- www.facebook.com/HelpAReporter
- www.facebook.com/ProfNetOnFB
- www.facebook.com/PitchRate
- www.facebook.com/mediadiplomat
- www.facebook.com/publiseek
- www.facebook.com/sourcebottle

"Like" their pages, and you'll be able to follow their query requests on your personal Facebook timeline.

Tip #48
Make a Connection

LinkedIn groups is another way to receive alerts about journalist queries. Of the companies listed above, both Media Diplomat and ProfNet have active groups, but only Media Diplomat really uses theirs to post media queries. You can find their group here: http://linkd.in/1cQf1x8.

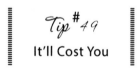

Tip #49
It'll Cost You

I have shared many ways to gain access via free media query services, but if you want a more customized service, there are paid options as well. All the media coverage I have earned was done using free services. However, there are some additional perks if you upgrade:

HARO Premium—For $149/month, HARO offers a paid service that allows you to customize which queries you receive and also alerts you ahead of time via email or text that a unique query matching your criteria is on its way. You can create a bio that is sent with your response, as long as you respond from within the HARO site versus responding from your email.

You are able to select keywords that are filtered, and queries with those keywords occasionally arrive before the regularly scheduled HARO email, so it gives you a bit of a head start over everyone else who might be responding.

ProfNet—ProfNet also offers a paid service ($950 annually plus a PR Newswire Membership is required— annual fee of $195) for which you receive media opportunities/queries from journalists sent directly to you in a daily email.

Queries are organized by industry and subject, allowing you to filter them based on your desired interest.

You can also offer your expertise and story ideas directly to the media using ProfNet Alerts. An Expert Alert is a three-sentence story idea that summarizes an expert's perspective on a timely issue or trend and alerts reporters to an expert's availability. A Daily Topic Alert is a group of experts who are available to comment on a timely, ongoing, or breaking news story. Both Expert Alerts and Daily Topic Alerts are transmitted over the wire to over 4,000 US news organizations and sent by email to over 7,000 registered reporters.

Responding to all of these queries might seem as if it is a great deal of work, but it's not. The initial set up, connecting, and linking takes a little bit of time. However, quick scans and searches take no time at all, and you'll get really good at skimming queries.

TAKE IT AWAY

It is in your moments of decision that your destiny is shaped.

—Tony Robbins

Important take-aways from this section are:

1. Set up boilerplate responses to various queries. You'll basically create your boilerplate responses as you answer new queries. I save mine in a separate email folder so, when a similar query comes in, I copy and paste the content and just edit the name and any specifics.
2. Sign up for the media query services and connect with them on their various social media outlets.
3. Always include your contact information.

Becoming
Print-worthy

The important thing is somehow to begin.

—Henry Moore

e were sitting in Panera Bread in the midst of our interview when the reporter asked me, "Why haven't you submitted this story before? This is so great!" I looked at her dumbfounded. I live in the Washington D.C. area. I've submitted story ideas to the *Washington Post* over and over again, but this was the first time a reporter responded. That's when she gave me the scoop on how things really work in the back room of newspapers. I've come to find the same holds true with local television too.

When you send a press release to the general fax number or the general email box of a media outlet, it could be any one of a number of reporters or producers who sees it. You never know who might like the idea and who won't. Just because one person passes on it doesn't mean it won't eventually get covered.

I sent in a story idea for National Inventor's Month in May that happened to catch this reporter's eye. I submitted my product various ways to the *Post* the year prior, but no one had ever bitten. She had never seen any of my press releases or story ideas before. She happened to notice this one and contacted me for the interview.

It was my persistence that landed a story about my business in the *Washington Post*. I kept developing new angles and finally found the right connection.

In this section I'll share other tips to help you increase your chances of being covered in a newspaper or magazine.

Tip #50

Are You the One?

Is there a particular magazine in which you see yourself or your product? Make sure you know who reads the magazine and that your topic or story resonates with them and also fits the style of the magazine.

This research can easily be done on Google by searching the publication name and the word "demographics." If you see a fit, either buy a copy of it or visit your local library and read the entire magazine.

Read the magazine as if you had written it, versus reading it for pleasure.

Try to gain the perspective of the magazine and what they are trying to portray to their readers.

Ask yourself:

- What content or topics area featured in the magazine?
- To whom are they writing?
- What is the feel of the magazine?
- Do you easily visualize your product, story, or business in that publication?
- Is there a particular segment in which your story fits?

If you can answer these questions and they pertain to you or your business, then it's time to formulate your story idea.

The same holds true for a newspaper, but it's really about what section you fit? Metro or Local? Lifestyle? Travel? Business?

Now that you've decided on the publication and the section, it's time to write a great story idea.

Tip #*51*
Make It Epic!

Do not go where the path may lead, go instead where there is no path and leave a trail.
—Ralph Waldo Emerson

The key to PR is having a great story to tell. Nobody likes a boring story. Make your story exciting or interesting. Share something you would want to know about.

A popular method of submitting to a magazine or newspaper is to provide a list of ideas or tips.

For example:

An interior designer might submit: *5 Tips for Decorating a Dorm Room for Under $50*

A realtor might submit: *The Top 3 "Bang-for-your-Buck" Upgrades to Sell Your House*

A relationship expert might submit: *7 Ways to "X" Your Ex!*

Take your expertise and turn it into a list with a really great headline and hook.

Another popular story idea is one that is alarming. For example, a story idea I submitted with great success was "WARNING: Kids Might Want to Break Their Foot to Wear This."

Can you cause controversy with your topic? This concept is another great way to get coverage. My friend, Bryan Toder, The No Fear Guy, www.thenofearzone.com, gets quite a bit of exposure with his story idea of: *Nicotine is not an addiction and I can prove it by asking you one simple question.* You're hooked, right? You want to know *what* the question is.

What's your story? Do you have something compelling you can share? Why did you start your business? What's the human element you can share about your story that would engage readers?

I know a fellow entrepreneur, Connie Griffith, who manufactures and distributes delicious sauces and mixes.

Recently, I learned her *story.*

Connie's husband, Ron, was the family chef. He was known among their friends and family for creating amazing sauces and was being encouraged by everyone to market his products. Sadly, he was stricken with ALS. He knew he had limited time, so he taught Connie all of his recipes and how to make the sauces. After he passed, she created a company in his honor to bring his dream alive and now runs a successful business, Gator Ron's Zesty Sauces and Mixes, named in his honor (and his alma matter, University of Florida), www.gatorrons.com. A portion of all sales' proceeds go to the Robert Packard Center for ALS Research at Johns Hopkins.

That is Connie's *story*, one that is much more appealing to the audience than just a company that makes sauces.

As for formatting your story idea, make it concise, on target, and easy to read, with a visual if possible. If there are statistics to back your story, use them. Always make sure you show the editor why he or she should cover this story. Show them how it benefits their audience.

EXPERT TIP

Be radically helpful to your editor! Put yourself in her shoes. Think the way she thinks. What problem does she have that you could solve? What do her readers want and need? Put a ton of value in that first contact, and you'll be really well positioned for that coveted call back.

—**Gay Edelman,** Former Senior Editor, Family Circle Magazine, Writer, Editor, Writing Coach, www.coachgay.com.

Tip #52
What's Newsworthy When?

In general, the calendar year is broken down into certain topics the media covers. Try to gear your story ideas to these seasonable trends.

The first quarter of the calendar year is geared towards New Year's resolutions. Many stories and articles are about weight loss and fitness and how to reach those goals as well as getting organized in the new year.

The second quarter is geared towards summer: travel, fashion, and summer fun.

The third quarter is a very slow news time and many reporters are very accessible. This time of year is great to present a new product or service. Also, if you have anything pertinent for Back-To-School, submit it at this time.

The end of the year is the biggest news time with everyone reflecting back on the year, so it's very difficult to get coverage this time of year. Can you do a Top 10 list of the year based on your expertise?

Tip #53

Timely Trends

Think about things that happen throughout the year to which you might be able to tie a story:

- Super Bowl Sunday
- Valentine's Day
- St. Patrick's Day
- Tax Day
- Mother's or Father's Day

- Independence Day
- The World Series

It's important to be creative and think outside of the box.

Tip #*54*
Be Non-Traditional

I want all my senses engaged. Let me absorb the world's variety and uniqueness.

—Maya Angelou

There is something known as the non-traditional calendar. This calendar lists unique holidays that have been established over time and can hopefully help spark creative ideas for submitting story ideas.

Use this calendar to help you think outside of the box and come up with unique story ideas to increase your chances of being covered in the media.

Some listed unique holidays include:

- Chicken Soup for the Soul Day
- National Simplify Your Life Week
- National Cell Phone Courtesy Month
- Business Women's Day
- Customer Service Week
- Safe Toy and Gift Month

Come up with some creative ways to tell your story, in a non-traditional way, for a better chance of gaining coverage in the media.

MY FAVORITE TIP

I submitted a story on Healthy Foot Month in April and appeared on the local _FOX_ news in Washington, D.C. Additionally, a submission for National Inventor's Month in May led to a story in the _Washington Post_. I recently saw a bakery that submitted an idea for a segment for National Bacon Day. There were several bacon products including their cupcakes with bacon sprinkles.

Tip #55
What's Old is New Again

The past cannot be changed; the future is still in your power.

—Hugh White

Do you have an old box of magazines in your attic or basement? Maybe even some of last year's editions in a magazine rack or on your coffee table? Get some inspiration from stories that have already been written. Just tweak an idea or article title and make it current. If someone wrote about it then, why not refresh it and submit the new and improved version?

Tip #56
Celebrity Sells

I see stardom very clearly as a construct that's been created in order to sell things.

—Julie Christie

Even if you have no connection to a celebrity, can you tie something they do or have done to your business?

As I mentioned earlier, I have an acquaintance, Rich Moore, www.richmooreinc.com, who belongs to a country club nearby in Virginia that was recently purchased by Donald Trump. He watched as the club was being renovated and admired the business practices of Mr. Trump. He wrote an article and subsequent press release entitled: *What I Learned from Donald Trump*. He did not know Donald Trump, he just watched how he worked on the project.

That article was covered in many publications and also resulted in Donald Trump calling Rich to discuss the article. In their conversation, Donald Trump even said to him, "You know you got so much coverage because you used my name?" Absolutely—celebrity sells! If you can tie in an "A-list" celebrity to your story, I highly recommend it.

Tip #57
Be a Star

There is a service called Contact Any Celebrity, www.contactanycelebrity.com. This site is a great resource to find celebrities. Contact Any Celebrity provides contact information for celebrities, pubic figures, agents, managers, publicists, and entertainment companies. Their database has information for over 100,000 people. This is a paid service, but they offer a free trial service, so if you have a list of celebrities for whom you want to obtain contact information, try the free service. If you think contacting celebrities will be something you need to do on a regular basis, sign-up.

MY FAVORITE TIP
I have been able to find most celebrities' contact information just by using Google.

Tip #58
Don't Pitch a Pitch

You hear the word "pitch" all the time, but what I found interesting when interviewing people in the industry is many of them don't want to be "pitched." Instead, why not be different? "Share" your story idea with an editor or reporter versus "pitching your pitch."

Tip #59
Best of the Best

Here is a listing of the Top 25 Magazines by circulation[1]. If you want to get the most *bang for your buck*—which, in this case, is *free*—try submitting to a magazine with a bigger circulation first.

It will be harder to break into these magazines, but why not try? My motto is, "Go Big or Go Home."

---

1   2011 figures—Source: nyjobsource.com

AARP The Magazine	22,395,670
AARP Bulletin	22,236,671
The Costco Connection	8,489,821
Better Homes and Gardens	7,648,900
Game Informer	5,954,884
Reader's Digest	5,653,440
National Geographic	4,445,603
Good Housekeeping	4,336,711
Woman's Day	3,863,710
Family Circle	3,816,958
People	3,556,753
Time	3,376,226
Ladies' Home Journal	3,267,239
Taste of Home	3,235,718
Sports Illustrated	3,207,861
Cosmopolitan	3,032,211
Prevention	2,903,417
Southern Living	2,830,179
AAA Via Magazine	2,732,291
Maxim	2,530,440
AAA Living	2,477,127
O, The Oprah Magazine	2,461,464
AAA Going Places	2,395,996
American Legion Magazine	2,323,308
Glamour	2,304,146

Tip #60

Don't Forget the Little Guy

Of course you want to get coverage in a national publication just for mass-exposure but that doesn't mean to only try there. Your success rate will be much higher in local and trade publications. Definitely submit your ideas to them as well. If you are covered in a trade or local publication, use that as a stepping stone to show a national publication a trend. Pull together similar articles about your type of business and use those to support showing a trend in your industry. Submit a story idea with regards to that and how you can speak to the trend.

Tip #61
Take Flight

One of the most captive audiences can be found on an airplane. Doesn't everyone at least flip through the in-air magazine from the seat back pocket at some point during their flight? Over 800 million people flew on airlines servicing the U.S. in 2012. That's a lot of eyes.

Submitting to an in-flight magazine is a very similar process to submitting to a regular publication. However, it is important to note that these types of magazines are looking for compelling long reads. Often their articles are several pages. So a tips list or "best of" idea will likely not be accepted for an in-flight magazine. You might be better served reaching out to a freelance writer who has written for one of these publications before, and submitting your story idea to them.

Also note that many of the in-flight magazines have an 8-month lead-time so it's important to plan way ahead if you are interested in submitting a story idea to an in-flight magazine.

CNN ranked the *Top 12 Best Airline Magazines*:

1) En Route (Air Canada), enroute.aircanada.com
2) Open Skies (Emirates, United Arab Emirates), www. openskiesmagazine.com
3) KiaOra (Air New Zealand), www.bauermedia. co.nz/Magazines/kiaora-air-new-zealand-inflight-magazine.htm
4) Sky (Delta, US), deltaskymag.delta.com
5) Indwe (SA Express, South Africa), www. freemagazines.co.za/index.php/our-magazines/indwe
6) Voyager (British Midland International, United Kingdom), www.voyagermagazine.com.au/current-issue/voyager-magazine
7) Smile (Cebu Pacifici, Phillippines), www.cebusmile. com
8) Qantas (Australia), www.bauer-media.com.au/ qantas_the_australian_way.htm
9/10) (tie)—Holland Herald (KLM, Netherlands), holland-herald.com
   Lufthansa Magazine (Germany), www.lhm-lounge. de
11) Go (Air Tran, US), www.airtranmagazine.com
12) Ryanair Magazine (Ireland), www.ryanair.com/en/ inflightmagazine

Based on audited and reported circulation numbers,[2] the *Top 10 Airline In-flight Magazines* in the U.S.:

---

2   Source: Cision

1) Sky, <u>deltaskymag.delta.com</u>
2) Hemispheres, <u>www.hemispheresmagazine.com</u>
3) Southwest Airlines Spirit, <u>www.spiritmag.com</u>
4) American Way, <u>hub.aa.com/en/aw/americanway</u>
5) US Airways Magazine, <u>www.usairwaysmag.com</u>
6) American Airlines Nexos, <u>hub.aa.com/es/nx/nexos</u>
7) Celebrated Living, <u>hub.aa.com/en/cl/ celebratedliving</u>
8) Hana Hou!, <u>www.hanahou.com</u>
9) The Private Journey, <u>www.privatejourneymagazine. com</u>
10) Go, <u>www.airtranmagazine.com</u>

MY FAVORITE TIP

If you have a story idea that is associated with one of an airline's hub cities, try that angle when submitting your idea.

Tip #62
Plan Ahead

Plans are nothing; planning is everything.
—Dwight D. Eisenhower

Stories for national magazines are usually planned at least four months ahead. Plan your submissions accordingly. If you have a great Back-to-School story idea, you need to send that in no later than April.

Newspapers are planned about two weeks ahead, so they have more flexibility versus a national magazine.

Tip #63
It's Beginning to Look a Lot Like Christmas

It's one of the most coveted spots in a magazine, The Annual Holiday Gift Guide. It's so hard to think about Christmas in spring, but if you are trying to have a product featured in a Gift Guide, you'll need to send in your information in May or June. Most Gift Guides for major publications are already done by July.

There will be opportunities later in the year for regional publications and newspapers, but for any of the top magazines listed above, send in your ideas no later than the end of June for the best opportunity to be selected for the Gift Guide.

Tip #64
Mark Your Calendar

Every magazine has an "editorial calendar" that lists the stories and topics they are going to be writing about and featuring in future editions for the year. It's really geared towards advertisers, but it's a secret tool you can use to find out what's going to be in the magazine each month, so you can plan your story ideas accordingly.

As I mentioned above, magazines have closing dates for content that usually run about four months prior to the issue date, so again, plan your story ideas accordingly. Don't send something for the March issue in January. You'll never get in and it's a waste of everyone's time.

Know the editorial calendars and plan your stories around them for the most success. Google the magazine name and either "editorial calendar" or "media kit" to find their annual calendar. Using this resource will help ensure the ideas you are submitting are laser focused to that publication and match exactly what they are looking for and when they need it.

MY FAVORITE TIP
Go through all of the magazines' editorial calendars in which you are interested and create your own calendar. Mark when and to whom you will need to submit your idea for the best chance of getting covered.

Tip #65
Be Timely

Is there something going on in the news for which you can provide expert opinion? This is your chance. If a reporter has written a story or article and you can add to their information, reach out to them. The same holds true for television. If you see a segment and you have additional information, reach out to that reporter or producer. they may do a follow-up and include you. Even if that is not the case, but they do respond, you have now gained a media contact. Start cultivating that relationship.

Tip #66
Who To Send It To

Are you an expert in your field? Can you provide relevant content on various topics? The media always need resources to whom they can turn. Why not become the expert in your field?

It is critical to know who the right contact person is at every media outlet pertaining to your subject matter. If your expertise is finance, don't send your story to the beauty editor. Find the person who writes articles or is the editor of a section related to your expertise. This person is the one with whom you want to start building a relationship.

Finding the right person will take a little bit of research, but thanks to Google, you should be able to find the information.

Another trick is to visit your local library and look at the mastheads of newspapers and magazines to find out who the contact person is for your area of expertise.

For newspapers, find out who is generally writing about your topic. Can you provide an alternative angle? Can you create controversy over something they've written about?

Connect with that reporter on social media and comment on articles they've already written. Be sure to mention what you might know about the subject. Start building a rapport with the reporter and developing a relationship. You might just be the next person they turn to when writing on that topic.

Tip #67

Digging For Gold

So now you know who to contact. How do you find them?

Many of the more mainstream magazines are part of a larger umbrella publishing company such as, Conde Naste, Hearst, Meredith, or Time.

Most large organizations have a common email thread. If you can find one person in the organization (this research is very easy with Google), you will likely be able to figure out your desired contact's email address. Some email thread examples are:

- Conde Nast Publications: firstname_lastname@ condenast.com
- Heart Publications: firstnamelastname@hearst.com
- Meredith Publications: firstname.lastname@ meredith.com
- Time Publications: firstname_lastname@timeinc. com

If you want to reach the editorial office of any of these, call the main switchboard at:

- Conde Nast, 212-286-2860
- Hearst, 212-649-2000
- Meredith, 515-284-3000
- Time, 212-522-1212

At PR for Anyone™ we offer a product with just over 2,300 email strings of television programs, magazines, and newspapers in both the U.S. and Canada. This list can be found at www.prforanyone.com/shop.

A great online resource to find publication information is www.mediabistro.com/mastheads. Type in the publication on which you are looking for information and scroll down to see their contact information including various editors names, mailing address, and email thread.

Another online resource is www.mastheadsonline. blogspot.com. This site lists several magazines and their contact information. However, double check any contacts listed as some have not been updated for sometime. A quick phone call to the number provided can verify if the person listed is still with the magazine.

Are they on social media? Connect with them. Follow them on Twitter. Engage with them. Respond to Facebook posts. Comment about articles they've written. Get to "know" them and *then* send them your idea. In today's electronic world, it really is easy to find and connect with people in the media.

If, however, you have the budget and want instant access to information, several companies have very comprehensive media resources and for a fee, you can access their databases. These are:

Vocus, www.vocus.com/software/#publicity

Cision, us.cision.com/media-database/media-database-
    overview.asp

Gebbie Press, www.gebbieinc.com/prices.htm

Easy Media List, www.easymedialist.com

Tip #68

I Know Where You Are

Mondotimes at www.mondotimes.com is an awesome resource for media contact information. This site can link you to the website of any television station, newspaper, magazine, or news radio station in the world.

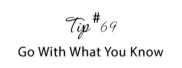

Tip #69
Go With What You Know

A trade publication is one of the best forms of PR because that is your target market with a fully engaged audience specifically interested in your topic.

For a listing of trade publications by industry, visit www.webwire.com/IndustryList.asp.

One of my first media placements was in a magazine called *Lower Extremity Review*. I submitted my product for review in their New Product section, and they published it. It was the perfect placement for CastMedic Designs because medical professionals focused on the lower leg read the magazine.

MY FAVORITE TIP
Not sure whom to approach? Find out where your competitors have gotten media coverage and start there.

Tip #70
Send a Special Package

If there is a media outlet that you really want to break into, consider packaging your idea and sending it in. A friend of mine, Romy Taormina, is the co-founder of Psi-Bands, www.psibands.com, a company that manufacturers fashionable nausea relief bracelets.

Psi-Bands landed a feature in *Oprah's O Magazine* when they sent one of their editors a package in the mail that delighted and offered the element of surprise. It was delivered in a white gift box with a gift tag on it that said, "Wrap up your nausea." No one could resist opening that up. Inside the gift box they included a few sets of Psi Bands and their brochure. The magazine feature was entitled *Grace Under Pressure* and was included on *Oprah's List* of favorite things.

Tip #71
A Side Job

Do you have a story to tell? Many magazines accept articles from freelancers and even pay for them. From writing about your topic for a business publication to the story behind your business, if it's compelling for a publication, there are places you can have an article published. Visit www.writersmarket.com for resources on freelancing.

Many publications also have guidelines for freelance articles on their website.

MY FAVORITE TIP

I submitted an article entitled *5 Tips for DIY PR* to American Business Magazine that was published. Freelancing is a great way to share your knowledge or your story in a way that is not self-promotion. Of course I received a by-line in the article, so my bio and website were included.

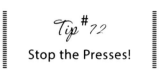

Tip #72

Stop the Presses!

A great website that lists every newspaper in the country is www.usnpl.com.

From this site, you are able to link to any newspaper and find contact information.

It is important to remember though, as much as we would all love to start out with a big feature in the Wall Street Journal, that probably isn't going to happen.

The easiest newspaper to score exposure with is your local paper. Most community papers will cover a new business, especially if you can come up with a unique hook.

Find the reporter or reporters who cover your topic and approach them directly.

From there, continue trying with regional and then national papers in your area.

The Crown Jewel
of Media

Enthusiasm is the yeast that makes your hopes shine to the stars. Enthusiasm is the sparkle in your eyes, the swing in your gait, the grip of your hand, the irresistible surge of will and energy to execute your ideas.

—Henry Ford

*Y*ou might be reading this book thinking to yourself, "Maybe she just got lucky. The average person isn't going to appear on national television. It's not realistic."

I have watched an acquaintance of mine, Elizabeth Lombardo, go from appearing on local television shows in her native Chicago to becoming a regular expert on the *Today Show.* I spoke with her recently because I wanted to share her story with you, to show that it really can be done, at any stage in your career.

Elizabeth is a clinical psychologist who specializes in happiness and is the author of the book, *A Happy You: Your Ultimate Prescription for Happiness.* When I asked her how her journey to the *Today Show* came about, she told me it had happened almost two years to the day of sending in new ideas to them, every month. Finally, one producer forwarded her idea to another, and that's when it started. The new producer reviewed her reel (we'll discuss reels later in this section), and invited her to appear on the show.

She consistently submitted story ideas with regular good content, but it took a full two years to receive a response. It took time, patience, and perseverance. She was willing to stay committed and put in the effort, and it paid off—she is now a regular guest on the *Today Show.*

Her story is the crux of how PR success is built, through relationships and perseverance. If one thing doesn't work, try again with something else.

Tip #73
It All Starts Here...

A goal properly set, is halfway reached.

—Zig Ziglar

Landing a spot on national television is often referred to as the "crown jewel" of media coverage. It is important to understand, however, that it is highly (and I emphasize *highly*) unlikely that you will be asked to appear on national television as an expert without some local television experience under your belt. This notion holds true especially on a live program. The producers have to be sure you will make a good guest. They can't risk having someone on-air who might freeze or who does not speak clearly and knowledgeably on their topic.

Local television is your stepping stone to national television. Barring the top local television markets that can be a little harder to crack, it should be relatively easy to get a local television appearance if you have something newsworthy to share.

I am not saying you can't get on-air in a top market; just be prepared for it to be more difficult and take more time. If you happen to live or work in a smaller market share area, you will probably be able to land a spot on the air sooner than if you are in a larger market share area. The reasoning behind this logic is that the larger market share stations are receiving more story submissions than the smaller stations.

A news assignment editor at one of our local network affiliates (Washington, D.C., #9 market) shared with me that they receive over 500 press releases and story ideas by noon on any given day. Imagine how many the #1 market in New York receives!

During my first year in business, I was able to land spots on both *NBC* and *FOX* in Washington, D.C., so it can be done. And Elizabeth, who we discussed earlier, regularly appears in the #3 market of Chicago. It just takes a little extra creativity because you are going up against a great number of other people vying to get coverage in a top television market.

If you are trying to get on a smaller market station that is not local to you, tie your story into something local in that area. Perhaps you went to school there, worked for a locally based company, or can specifically help people in that area? A local station is going to want a local angle. Get creative and discover what makes you newsworthy to them and their audience.

The Top 10 Local Television Markets are:

- New York
- Los Angeles
- Chicago
- Philadelphia
- Dallas-Ft. Worth
- San Francisco-Oakland-San Jose
- Boston
- Atlanta
- Washington, D.C.
- Houston

EXPERT TIP

At my very first job producing television at *The Oprah Winfrey Show,* I learned how to be uncompromising in my search for the most niche expert at the top of their industry with the most current and relevant information to add. Be that person. Have something unique to say. Personality is a must, must, must—you must engage me. If I don't want to listen to you, I can't expect millions of viewers to want to, right? I must respect and like you the minute I lay eyes on you or its over. So many experts today don't know how to present themselves—their walking brand—properly. My advice is threefold—know your brand inside out, know yourself and how you are being received, and understand how the television industry works—what producers are

looking for and how to fill that need—how you fit in to the solution.

—**Natalie Mashaal**, founder Mashaal Media Corp., www.nataliemashaal.com.

Tip # 74

Who, What, When, Where?

The first person to contact at a local news station is the assignment editor. They are the idea people with their fingers on the pulse of the community, and they are the ones who submit ideas up the ladder to production.

Due to the high number of submissions television stations receive, your idea will need to stand out in that sea of email. The first thing they see is the subject line of your email. Make it catchy so they want to read more. Next, make sure your email is short and easy to read. A wordy email will likely be deleted. They just don't have the time.

When submitting an idea, know where it fits into their programming. Many news programs do not have guests in their main news slots of 5:00 pm, 6:00 pm, and 11:00 pm, but check what they offer in terms of morning and/or mid-day shows and submit your ideas specifically for those programs.

Local news stations read local blogs and community papers to get ideas for their show, so if you are covered in any of these publications, use those stories when you send your idea to the local station. Local television stations really do want to feature local businesses and guests, but remember to be creative with your ideas so it's something easy for them to work with and appealing to their viewers.

Tip #75
Your "Sizzle"

We are all of us stars, and we deserve to twinkle.
—Marilyn Monroe

Once you've garnered a few local media appearances, it's important to put those together into a media reel, also known as a "sizzle reel." This video is a short montage of you on television discussing your expertise. A reel can easily be created with programs such as iMovie on your computer. There are also companies who specialize in creating these reels, such as my fabulous production company, Acerbic Entertainment, www.acerbicfilm.com. You can also look for freelancers on Craig's List. Or, if you have a university close by with a film school, see if you can get a student to help you.

Tip #76
Make It Easy For Them

If you don't tell your story, someone else will.
—Unknown

Make it easy for a producer by providing a full layout of how you envision the segment will go. Refer back to TIP #31, where we show you an easy email layout to use when submitting your segment idea. Come up with a catchy hook that they can use to introduce the segment. If you are submitting to a national television station, include your sizzle reel as well. As always, keep it simple and easy to read. Make it easy for the producer to visualize the segment.

Tip #77
Be Our Guest

Many of the syndicated talk shows have a "Be on the Show" section on their website. Listed here will be topics they are covering or guests needed for future segments. If you fit into a category for which they are requesting guests, submit using the online form. These are frequently updated so check back often. Here are a few examples from current top rated shows:

www.ellentv.com/be-on-the-show

www.steveharveytv.com/be-on-the-show

http://www.rachaelrayshow.com/show-info/be_on_the_show/

Every season there are new talk shows popping up. Set a Google Alert to keep you posted on new shows. You will have a better chance appearing on a new show that is trying to fill their shows than a top rated established show. Once you know about the new shows, don't forget to check their "Be a Guest" section.

MY FAVORITE TIP
The television production industry is actually quite small. Most of the associate and senior producers all know one another. When a talk show is canceled, many of those producers move to one of the new shows that are replacing the canceled show. This is why building relationships is

such an important component of PR. I met a producer who was working on Anderson Cooper's daytime show right before it was canceled. She is now working on one of the new shows. I have been in touch with her about appearing on that show. Always keep your doors open.

Tip #78
Check the Classifieds

Talk shows filmed in New York, Chicago, and Los Angeles often post guest queries on Craig's List. National shows have travel budgets, so they often try to find guests in their production cities to cut down on those costs. Don't let geography stop you from reaching out to them. I am located in Washington, D.C. so the trip to New York is relatively short. For a national appearance on a show taping in New York, it is worth it for me to pay my own travel expenses. If the opportunity arises to appear on a national show and you are not local to them, offer to pay the travel expenses for your first appearance.

Tip #79
HARO-ing for TV

Starting in August, until around April, many nationally syndicated shows put out guest requests on HARO. Most of these shows are on hiatus over the summer and don't film. But come August, they are frequently searching for guests on various topics, and the producers are in a hurry to fill segments. This time of year is a great time to monitor HARO closely to see if there is a fit.

Tip #80
Social "Networking"

Make connections with television shows you are interested in appearing on through social media. They often post guest requests on both Facebook and Twitter. Stay active in discussions on these sites as well, as you might catch the eye of a producer working on a particular segment.

www.facebook.com/ellentv
www.facebook.com/SteveHarveytv
www.facebook.com/TheRachaelRayShow

For Twitter, I recommend finding particular producers, following them, and interacting directly. The hosts themselves don't do any booking and keep in mind, you probably aren't going to have much luck interacting with Ellen DeGeneres and her over 20 million Twitter followers.

Tip #81
Where Do I Find You?

And, when you want something, all the universe conspires in helping you to achieve it.
—Paulo Coelho, The Alchemist

If appearing on television is your dream, watch the program you would like to be on and become aware of their format so your story ideas are on-target. You can often find individual producer information at the end of the show in the credits. Another way to find out this information is to simply Google the segment name and topic and look for the name of the producer via your search. Keep in mind that television talk shows have multiple producers, so if one does not respond, try another.

Many television producers are on LinkedIn. With the regular LinkedIn membership it is difficult to reach out to them blindly (and frowned upon by LinkedIn), so look for a mutual connection. If you don't have one, it might be worth upgrading to a premium account for a month or more to try to connect. LinkedIn often offers a free month trial of their premium service.

Remember, producers are looking for you. They have the daunting task of coming up with new material daily. You have information they may want and need. Most producers I have reached out to have accepted my LinkedIn invitation to connect. I then become another potential resource for them.

One important thing to learn about is the hierarchy of television. Although the producer is the top of the totem pole, your best bet is to actually build a relationship with an intern or production assistant. They are on the pulse of what's hot and trending, and they submit their ideas to the producer. They are also tasked by the producer to find good guests and experts.

Interns and production assistants are the ones with whom you want to connect. They are working toward being a producer some day, so you are continuing to build good future relationships.

They are usually younger people and very active on social media. Find them on Twitter and, if they have a Facebook page affiliated with their television show, connect there. Do not try to connect with them personally on Facebook unless you have built a relationship with them and have become friends.

For local television, pick up the phone and call the station. Ask them which producer covers your topic. Business… Fashion…Health…and ask for their email address. It's really that easy!

Tip #82
No Stalking Please

I have heard repeatedly in my interviews with television producers that follow-up communication is okay. Please don't hound them though, and don't continue to submit the same idea over and over, trying to convince them how great the idea is. You never want to imply to a producer that they are not doing their job.

Producers are very busy and most shows are on tight budgets, so these producers are over-worked as it is. Try an email follow up. If it's a time-sensitive idea on a current hot story, give them a call. If they don't respond, wait a month or so and submit another story idea.

MY FAVORITE TIP

Do not contact producers while they are on the air or during taping. Obviously, you know when live shows are

on-air. For other shows, call the main number and ask when they tape. Show them you respect their position and email or call producers during their off-air time.

Tip #*83*
Pay To "Play"

Pay-to-play is also known as entertainment branding. Basically, you pay someone who has the contacts in the industry to guarantee placement on a television show. Very rarely would this exposure be on the *Today Show* or *Good Morning America* and if so, it would be extremely expensive. Think of it more as advertising, since you are paying to have you or your business/product featured on a television show.

It is extremely important to look at the return on investment if you go this route. If, for example, you sell ski apparel and your contact has placement capability in Florida, is that really a good idea? Research the markets and the company doing the placing. Make sure it is a good fit and the investment is worth the exposure you will get out of the appearance.

Tip #*84*
It's All About You

Eighty percent of success is showing up.

—Woody Allen

You've done all the work I mentioned here and it finally happens, you get a television appearance! Now what? The scariest part about your first television appearance is not knowing what to expect. It's the fear of the unknown. I want to take some of the mystery out of it for you, so you can relax and enjoy it, because it really is a lot of fun.

Many segments are aired live but the producer should let you know whether you will be live or taped. Even if it's taped, the show often does not want to edit it, so I recommend you act as if it's live.

If the show does not provide transportation to the studio, they will tell you what time to arrive. Make sure you are on time. You can't keep live television waiting.

When you arrive, the production assistant or associate producer will take you to the "green room" (waiting room or lounge) before going on-air. If it's a national show, the room usually has yummy treats. (Of course, on your first appearance, you'll probably be too nervous to eat anything.) Most national programs provide hair and makeup, so you wait in the green room until the associate producer comes to get you. If it's a local show, you should be ready to go on-air when your producer or host arrives.

Turn your cell phone off. I was surprised how small the actual television studios are, and it is important to watch your noise level as they are likely filming something else while you are preparing for your segment.

A sound tech will come in to microphone (mic) you. There is a small transmitter that attaches to your backside, and a wire they will run from the transmitter, under your clothes, and clip to your lapel. A very important note, when you are mic'ed, the sound people on the other end can hear everything you are saying and doing. Make sure you use the restroom before they put your microphone on, and be careful of what you say because someone is listening on the other end.

Most television appearances are conversational, so don't worry about talking into a specific camera. The host will likely use the teleprompter and introduce you. It's okay to look at the camera/teleprompter then too, but then adjust to your host. You can always ask them before you air where they want you to look.

Usually the host will be prepared with questions and guide the interview, but you should always be prepared for the host who isn't ready for the segment. Be ready to talk about your topic for three to four minutes, which is the average time for a television segment.

This scenario happened to me in one of my first television interviews. I had to literally take over the interview, and luckily it ended up fine, but always be prepared for things not to go as anticipated.

Prepare yourself ahead of time for the host who is passive, the host who is antagonistic (how can you guide it to be more positive?), or the host who asks non-relevant questions. (We'll address these situations later in this section.)

Some tips while on camera:

- Be warm, approachable and sincere.
- Know your topic.
- If standing, don't lock your knees, relax.
- If possible, keep your feet on the floor so you don't swing your feet.
- Keep your hands in your lap or rest them on the arm of the chair.

- Be comfortable.
- Don't cross your arms.
- Always Smile. Even with a serious topic, a sympathetic, thoughtful smile gives you a human connection.
- Most of the daytime variety shows are looking for guests with lots of passion and energy.
- Don't get up until the producer tells you to do so.

The host should mention the name of your company at some point during the interview. If the host does not, and you can find a way to interject it, doing it once is okay. Remember your job is to serve their audience, not yourself, so repeatedly saying your company name is a good way to *not* get invited back.

It is not appropriate to give your website address on-air unless specifically asked. You should also check if they will be running your information on a news ticker during your interview. If so, make sure you provide the show with this information to ensure accuracy.

Lastly, be a courteous guest that they will want to invite back. If you act as if you are a prima donna and should be treated as such, I can almost guarantee they won't want to have you back. I always leave my television appearances with big hugs and thank you's to everyone, which is much more appreciated than an entitled attitude.

EXPERT TIP
What is the biggest blunder a guest can make? Making it all about them, rather than meeting the needs of the audience. The interviewee keeps saying their company name, their book, their product, their website. It

annoys the heck out of a reporter. And, rambling with no solid sound bites. People get nervous and don't speak coherently. Three sentences, then they're done. Relationship is the name of the game, hence the interview is a conversation, not a one-sided monologue.

—**Shawne Duperon**, Media Coach & Trainer, 6-Time EMMY® Award Winner, www.shawnetv.com.

Tip #*85*
Learning to Talk

A sound bite is a succinct way to get your message across. An average sound bite is about five to eight seconds and covers what you want to say about one specific point. Speaking in sound bites is important for both television and radio because it prevents rambling and incoherency in the interview.

Watch the interview I did with Charlotte Graham, veteran television producer and founder of 360° Speaking, for Expert's Corner at www.prforanyone.com/experts-corner. In her response on speaking in sound bites, she unintentionally answered in sound bites. It's a great way to learn how to use them.

Tip #*86*
Ya'll Come Back Now

If a man be gracious and courteous to strangers, it shows he is a citizen of the world.

—**Francis Bacon**

So now you've made it. You've been a guest. How do you keep getting asked back? Of course, most importantly is to be a good guest. We've heard from many of our experts in Expert's Corner at www.prforanyone.com/experts-corner how important authenticity is. You have to be able to relate to the audience. Have energy. Get your message out and be excited about it. Be comfortable on camera so you don't come across as unauthentic or unbelievable.

"Be nice to everyone" is my motto at home with my kids. I have instilled that value in them since the early days of playgroups. Elizabeth, who we discussed earlier, mentioned this philosophy too. Be nice to the page who walks you down the hall. Be nice to the makeup artist who makes you look fabulous on-air. Be nice to the assistant producer who gets you ready for your interview. How you treat people at the show goes a long way in determining whether or not they want you back.

Lastly, be accessible and available to them when they need you. Respond immediately to emails and if they need you in-studio tomorrow, drop everything and say, "Of course!" Be the type of guest they need, someone who can accommodate their crazy production schedules.

Tip #87
Worst-Case Scenario

When we face the worst that can happen in any situation, we grow.

—Elisabeth Kubler Ross

When doing a television interview, it is vital that you are fully prepared for anything. Would you know what to do if your host wasn't prepared for your segment? You have to be able to confidently take control of the interview and make sure you can bring it back to the topic. What if a host is speaking on and on and you can barely get a word in? Are you self-assured enough to find a break in the conversation and share your message? What if the host says your name or your company name wrong? How do you rectify this situation? Maybe they are just having a bad day and it takes its toll on your interview. Would you be able to handle any of these situations?

If you plan to be a regular expert on local television, and eventually national television, I recommend media training. Professionals will put you in these situations doing mock interviews and guide you through the appropriate responses. They can also help you put your message into succinct sound bites for various interviews whether it is the standard three to four minute interview or perhaps a longer one.

I recommend working with a media trainer who has significant television experience and can prepare you for any scenario. In the event you are placed in any of these situations and you rebound successfully, it adds to your credibility as a strong guest.

Tip #*88*
Looking Good

I learned about the need for television makeup the hard way. I had no idea that most local television stations don't have hair and makeup artists on staff. A local show in a top television market such as New York or Chicago might have a makeup artist, but even in Washington, D.C., the #9 market in the country, the local television stations don't provide this service.

Early on, I was on a local program in Texas and wore a white shirt and had on light makeup. I looked like a ghost! I wish someone had told me about the bright lights used in television studios and the need for heavier makeup than my everyday wear. Feel free to see what *not* to do with makeup when you land a television appearance, www.youtube.com/watch?v=bB3CoteD6BY.

The lights used in television studios are very bright and intense, and it is very important to wear the appropriate makeup. My best recommendation is to have your makeup done professionally, if at all possible. Find a local makeup artist or visit a store like M-A-C at your local mall, www.maccosmetics.com/locator/index.tmpl.

Often, however, local appearances are not scheduled until the very last minute. I got a call at 7:00 p.m. asking if I could be at the local *NBC* station by 9:00 a.m. the next morning. In that case, I had no way to schedule anything.

It is important to know how to apply your own television makeup, just in case. We were very fortunate to have Tracey Garcia, of *FOX News*, and a freelance makeup artist in the Washington, D.C. area, share television makeup tips in our Expert's Corner, www.prforanyone.com/experts-corner.

Men, you also need to think about makeup. The studio lights can make you look green. If you have facial hair, it is important to know how to cover that up a bit. Tracey offers a segment on men's makeup as well. Gentleman, learn what needs to be in your makeup bag.

Tip #89
What to Wear Where

Fashion fades, only style remains the same.

—Coco Chanel

You've got your TV makeup figured out. Now, what do you wear? The easiest thing to do is watch the show and see what the host and other guests are wearing and dress comparably. If you're on a business show, wear business attire, as you want to be taken seriously.

Make sure you are comfortable in whatever you are wearing. If not, it could affect how you hold yourself on camera. Remember, you want to appear relaxed, comfortable and authentic on television.

Avoid solid white, all black, and busy patterns. Find out if they use a green screen and if so, don't wear green. The same holds true if the news program regularly uses a blue background; don't wear blue.

Bright colors are great for TV. When you go an a national show, they will often ask you to bring several outfits, and then a wardrobe person will pick your outfit based on what the host is wearing and if there are other people in the segment as well.

For women, scarves and dangling jewelry are distracting and should be avoided. Men, don't wear short socks.

Tip #90
You Got the Axe

You learn how to be a gracious winner and an outstanding loser.

—Joe Namath

As heartbreaking as it is, getting bumped from a show happens. Don't take it personally. This scenario is somewhat common on live television, especially if there is breaking news. It can also happen at the last minute when a segment is canceled in favor of something else or a decision is made to run another segment longer.

The most important thing you can do when this situation happens is to remain gracious. Your ultimate goal is to be invited back, and if you come off irritated or angry with the producer, you will likely not be invited back for a future segment.

The television production world is very small, and the last thing you would want is to be blacklisted as a difficult guest. Be thankful and appreciative, and remember that you now have a relationship with this producer so you can continue to offer future segment ideas.

I'll share my national television heartache…I was asked to send a decorated medical boot to a national morning show, and the segment was booked. I watched and waited with nervous anticipation. The hour kept ticking away, and then the show ended, no CastMedic Designs. I had officially been bumped. Although it still hasn't aired, I am in touch with the producer regularly. The good news is I've built a relationship with that producer and have responsive email conversations with her. And, she has asked to hang on to the boot for a future segment, so I stay in touch and hope for my big morning show break.

Copy That

Make sure you know a local videographer who can record any of your television appearances. Use this footage on your website and to gain more media exposure. Most shows will allow you to use your segment on your own social media sites and in future marketing. However, some will not and have strict copyright rules, so make sure you know their policies and only use footage you are permitted to share. Many shows now post video clips directly to YouTube and, if that is the case, you are permitted to use the footage for your personal distribution. Remember, once you land some media exposure, it will open your opportunities to more and continue to add to your credibility.

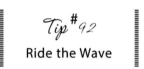

Ride the Wave

We must learn to apply all that we know so we can attract all that we want.

—Jim Rohn

You've worked and worked and you finally get a PR hit. Now what? Tell the world because media begets media.

After I taped the *Steve Harvey Show,* I had a few weeks before it aired. It airs on our local *NBC* affiliate, so I sent them a press release saying a local business would be on the show November 1st and would they want to cover it on the daytime news program before the *Steve Harvey Show* aired that day? It worked and they invited me to appear on the show. I filmed an entire segment all about my products, and they asked for a lot of visuals so I was able to bring every decorated boot I had. That gave me yet another television appearance and more credibility.

After Diana Ross was photographed wearing a CastMedic Designs' product, I contacted the producer of the *Steve Harvey Show* with whom I had worked. Steve Harvey ended up airing an entire segment on my company and me, to show how successful his Top Inventor was becoming. He said, "If THE Diva, Diana Ross, is wearing it, you know it has to be good!" And he showed the press photo of her wearing the product. This kind of exposure is priceless.

Remember to think outside of the box when you land media exposure. Consider who would be interested in knowing you appeared on a certain show or in a publication, and what you can spin from it.

Tip #93
What's Your Reality?

Reality is merely an illusion, albeit a very persistent one.
—Albert Einstein

Love it or hate it, reality television is here to stay. There are many PR opportunities in this realm. As I'm sure you know, "reality" television is actually quasi-scripted, so there are numerous possibilities for you or your business to be featured in a reality-themed show.

First and foremost, calculate the risk of reality television. You have no say in how you will be portrayed, so if there is any possibility that you or your product may not be presented in the best light, ask yourself what this depiction could mean for your business. There is the old adage of, "any publicity is good publicity," but you'll have to make that decision ahead of time. Look at famous reality television actors such as Snookie or Omarosa. Even with a negative image, they have become very well-known and successful.

On the other hand reality television can catapult fame. There is Elisabeth Hasselbeck who appeared on *Survivor*. She spent many years as a host of *The View* and is now on *Fox & Friends*. Or, Bethenny Frankel, who was on *Housewives of New York City*. She has since sold her Skinnygirl cocktail line for over 100 million dollars and is now hosting her own daytime talk show.

If you decide this medium is the route for you, the person to contact is the talent producer or the talent executive for that show. You can find those names in the credits at the end of the program. Just like a magazine or television story idea, prepare the same type of submission for reality television. Put a good creative idea together and submit it. You will probably want to include a video with your submission because of the nature of this type of programming and their need to see your personality on camera.

EXPERT TIP

Knock it out of the park on your audition reel. Make an impression so even if you don't get on that particular show, you'll end up in the producer's "Not This Show" file. Producers go from show to show and they keep files of great

people who have auditioned. You might end up on another show they are producing. — TaJuan "TeeJ" Mercer, best-selling author & Reality TV Coach www.iSeeMeOnTV. com. Author of *So You Want To Be On A Reality Show?: Insider Tips to Make the Cut*. She has worked on top reality shows such as, The Bachelor, Redneck Divas, Joan & Melissa, Swamp People, My Cat From Hell, LA Hair, and many others.

Tip #94

Becoming a Prop

Do you want to see your product on television? Is there a particular show or character on a show that you see using your product? If so, reach out to them! Again, it's really that easy.

The first thing to do is call the main network and ask for the number of the show you are trying to reach. Before you call the show directly, you'll need to know if you want the costume designer or the prop master. If it's clothing related (purses, jewelry, shoes, etc.), ask for the costume designer. For anything on set, ask for the prop master.

I keep telling you to pick up the phone because reaching someone in the media really is that easy.

Obviously, I have a very unique product, but I have spoken with the costume designers of all the major medical shows and emailed them information. If there is a storyline with someone in a medical boot, at least they know where to come to make it fashionable.

Here are the main numbers to all of the mainstream media companies.

ABC—212-456-7777
A&E—212-210-1400
BET—202-608-2000
CBS—818-655-5000/323-575-2211/310-575-7000
CW—818-977-2500
DISNEY CHANNEL—818-569-7500
E! ENTERTAINMENT—323-954-2400
FOX—310-369-1000
HBO—212-512-1000
LIFETIME—212-424-7000
NICKELODEON—212-258-7579
NBC—818-840-4444
USA/NBC UNIVERSAL—212-413-5000
WB—818-954-3000

Find out about new shows and television pilots at www.productionweekly.com.

EXPERT TIP

TV and movies tell stories about people and the clothing or decor needs to reflect their persona to get their character across to the audience. Be sure you have watched the TV show and are 100% sure your product "fits" the character you are going after. Once you are confident about it being a good match, calling will be so much easier.

—**Sarah Shaw**, www.Entreprenette.com.
Her handbags were seen in movies including,
Ocean's 11, *America's Sweethearts*, and *Legally Blonde*
and the television shows *Friends* and Will and Grace.

Working in
Your PJ's

Nothing is impossible, the word itself says "I'm possible."
—Audrey Hepburn

I love giving radio interviews. It's similar to chatting with a friend, hanging out while getting to share my expertise with thousands of listeners, all clueless that I'm having a hair-for-radio day. Radio is easier than TV because the audience cannot judge based on appearance. I've given radio interviews after working out, in my pajamas, with no makeup on and my hair in a ponytail.

Nevertheless, whether you're dressed to the nines for the camera or sporting a sweatsuit at the recording studio, remember, you're there to share your message, to be engaging.

Rambling, reciting, and monotonous monologuing will only inspire people to change the station.

Remember the sound bite (TIP #85)? It's even more important to be engaging on radio and allow your voice to provide visuals for the listener. Speak succinctly to get your point across. This technique is just as important with radio as it is with television.

If you think the only thing you'll be doing in your PJ's is dreaming of getting on the radio, think again.

Meet Jess Todfelt, a 2009 addition to the Guinness Book of World Records®, www.jesstodtfeld.com.

A former television producer and media training consultant, he co-wrote a book on business speaking. When it came time to promote his book, a friend remarked that because of his background, Jess should have no problem gaining tons of publicity, in fact, why not more publicity than anyone had ever gotten before?

Fueled by the friendly taunts, Jess set out to break the world record for the most radio interviews given in a 24-hour period. Game on! The number to beat…72.

Jess compiled a list of 2,000 talk radio stations, sending each program director a personalized email. The program director is the top of the food chain in radio so if he or she goes for it, you're in.

Specific lists of media contacts are available for purchase. You then take that information and import it into a mass-email program such as, Your Mailing List Provider, www.yourmailinglistprovider.com or Constant Contact, www.constantcontact.com that can address each email personally by their name.

And now… *The Art of the Hook.* So what did Jess email them? The first segment idea he sent said, "Your Show Can Be Part of a Guinness Record," followed by ten proposed show topics from which the station could choose.

As stations started signing up, he sent a second email that said, "40 stations have already signed up to break the record. Will you be next or left behind?"

When he hit 60 bookings, "We will easily hit the record of 72, will you be part of it?" By then he had people coming to him requesting to be number 73.

Jess went down in history, having signed up 112 stations, mainly news talk or drive time radio, in all 50 states, Puerto Rico, Guam, Portugal, Spain, and South America.

Tip #95
What's Your Story?

As with magazines and television, send a targeted segment idea to the radio program. It's not you, your product, or your book that the show is interested in, it's what you can offer to entertain their audience. Tailor the way you share your expertise so it will be compelling to them.

I have a product-based business, yet I'm always asked to do radio interviews. It's the story they love, that I had a vision, followed my passion, and brought my idea to fruition. Stories of getting a business off the ground through perseverance, and overcoming all the obstacles along the way, are inspiring. Hosts and audiences love these types of stories.

Follow the Rules

A radio interview is a television interview, minus the visuals. The rules of being interviewed on television hold true for radio as well. Be authentic. Know your topic. Speak in sound bites. Be a gracious guest and get invited back. By practicing what I preach, every radio interview I have ever done has resulted in an open invitation to return.

It's Free Here Too

We've already learned about the free query services such as HARO and SourceBottle, but there is also a website specific to radio queries, www.radioguestlist.com. Submit your information and once a day you receive radio queries of shows needing guests. Send in your concise, timely responses, and you will be on your way to becoming a regular radio guest.

How Do I Find You?

The easiest way to find radio stations is to Google the phrase "radio talk show" and "keywords related to your subject matter." Research the results for a good fit, then find the station's contact information using the methods I've outlined.

Larger, nationally syndicated shows have a staff of producers. The person you want to contact is the "booker." This is the producer who schedules the guest experts and authors.

Local, Internet, and Blog Talk shows may have just one producer and a host. Or, the host might handle everything, so there is only one person to contact.

You can also search www.radio-locator.com and radiostationworld.com, both excellent resources for finding radio shows.

Tip [#]*99*
For Starters

You don't have to be great to start, but you have to start to be great.

—Zig Ziglar

It's always a good idea, especially in your first few interviews, to ask if you can provide questions ahead of time. This way you will be completely prepared for the interview. Personally, I prefer not having preset questions so my interview can flow naturally. Some hosts and guests, however, prefer to go the prepared question route to make sure they have all bases covered.

If your interview is live, in-studio, always arrive early.

For a phone-in interview, always use a landline and disable call-waiting. You don't want to be mid-sentence when another call beeps in and cuts you out. Consider a headset as well. I gesture with my hands quite a bit when speaking, even on radio. It helps me articulate my story when I can walk and talk using both hands.

If you work from home, doing a radio interview is risky in terms of possible distractions or noise. If you have a dog, put your pup out of earshot. Put a sign by your doorbell asking people not to ring or knock during interview time. If your kids are home, remind them you are on a live call and cannot be distracted. (When my entire family is home, I often lock myself in the basement and tell them they can't come down.) Lastly, turn off anything in the house that could cause background noise such as your cell phone, a ceiling fan, the radio, and television.

MY FAVORITE TIP
Have some water nearby just in case your mouth gets dry. Nobody will see the water bottle or even know if you sneak a sip during the interview.

Tip # 100
Talk the Talk

Bring the best of your authentic self to every opportunity.
—Brian Jantsch

As I mentioned above, you might provide questions ahead of time. Be prepared with your responses, but don't use notes. You want to be authentic and conversational, not rehearsed. If you're asked a question that you don't know the answer to, say you don't know, instead of fumbling your way through uncharted waters. And never answer with just a "yes" or "no." Always add more to your response.

Be a compelling guest, but let the host lead the discussion. It is their show and the audience is tuned in to hear them interview you. You are there to teach, not sell. As with television, don't drop your company name or website over and over. There will be a time to do that. Not once has a host forgotten to let me talk about my company and give my website along with any other information I wanted to share. Hosts will always make time for this promotion.

Last but not least, keep an eye on the clock. Give yourself the last several minutes to wrap up and have time to share your business information. If it's an eight-minute interview, know you're wrapping up your content at six minutes. Most syndicated shows are either eight or fifteen-minute interviews, while Blog Talk is usually 30 minutes, sometimes even the full hour.

Content
is King

*I*f you're not blogging, start. If you think you're better off appearing on television or radio than having someone blog about you, think again. When you are covered in a blog, that post lives on eternally on the Internet. If you are fortunate enough to be covered in a top-ranking blog, it's even better because you get to piggyback on their top search engine optimization (SEO) ranking. When someone searches about your topic, and you were covered in a high-ranking blog, it will come up early in the Google search results. This is not necessarily the case with a television appearance or a quote in a magazine. Take advantage of the power of the blog and what it means for SEO and search results on the Internet.

Remember, bloggers need regular fresh content just like other media. They welcome the opportunity to blog about businesses, products, books, and interesting stories. Another option is to guest blog for them. A quick Google search using your industry keyword(s) and "blog" should help you find some great resources.

If you are a product-based business, be prepared to send review samples to bloggers. Many blogs are actually product review sites and are a great way to get exposure to a large audience. I was approached by a fashion blogger from Mercedes Benz Fashion Week in New York who was in a walker boot. I sent her product for her boot, and in return she sent me several photographs of herself with professional models and celebrities. We were able to create a great marketing campaign around Fashion Week.

As for your personal blog, the time is now. Content is king! The more written and video content you are putting on the Internet, the more secure your place is as the preeminent expert in your field. If the media is looking for an expert, they will likely Google the topic, and if you come up near the top, are branded well, and show that you have provided great content, the chances of them reaching out to you are significantly increased.

Tip[#] *101*
Let's Get This Party Started

You miss 100% of the shots you don't take.
—**Wayne Gretzky**

There is no excuse for not starting a blog. If technology is your issue, here are some resources to start a blog: <u>www.typepad.</u>

com, www.wordpress.com and www.blogger.com. There are plenty of free teaching resources available on e-How as well, to help you get started on any of these, www.ehow.com.

You know your subject matter. You started a business based on it. But if you need help getting creative, go back to the *Art of the Hook* section or use the various segment ideas we suggested. Writing a post of tips for others is a great way to start. Numbered lists such as, "The 5 Best Reasons To..." are easy to write. You don't have to reinvent the wheel with your blog. Go with what you know and consider doing some short videos you can post on your blog as well.

It's all about getting information out on the Internet and establishing yourself as *the* expert in your field.

Tip #102
Once is Enough

Post a blog article only once. Duplicate content must be avoided. If Google realizes you have uploaded the same information on various sites, they may lower your search engine optimization (SEO) rank. Write a post, upload it on your blog or contribute to another blog, and then move on to another topic.

Tip #103
Short and Sweet

Blog posts should be about 500 to 600 words. Readers enjoy blog posts that are short and to the point. Additionally, Google doesn't typically index past the first few hundred words or so in a blog post, so in terms of SEO, longer posts are a waste of time. Don't write based on the number of words but rather on content and what your readers will enjoy.

Tip # *104*
Be Unique

It is important to make sure your content is 100% original and that you understand copyright laws before blogging. Here is the link to the U.S. Government's Copyright Law website, www.copyright.gov/title17. If you have questions or concerns, contact an attorney.

A free resource available to test your blog post to make sure Google will see it as original content that is not plagiarized is Copyscape, www.copyscape.com. Copyscape will find any matches to existing content and let you know if what you've written is too similar to what someone else has already posted.

Tip # *105*
Social Butterfly

Make sure you have social media share buttons posted with each article so readers can easily tweet, post, and share them on social media sites. A simple plug-in to your blog website will allow you to add this feature.

Tip # *106*
Pay It Forward

Consider becoming a contributor on a high traffic blog. Your article will gain a great deal more exposure on a site with millions of viewers than your own blog site. A great place to start is, www.business2community.com/become-a-contributor. Anyone can apply to become a contributor with no prior blogging experience. To find blogs and information about them, go to www.technorati.com.

MY FAVORITE TIP
Do your research about the blog and determine how you could contribute and/or fill-in on any topics they have not yet covered.

Tip # *107*
Stats 101

Check out these blogging statistics:

- 81% of Internet consumers in the U.S. take advice and trust information from blogs.
- Most buyers will read an average of 11 consumer reviews prior to making a purchase.
- 77% of people who use the Internet read content on blogs.
- Of companies that blog, 57% of them have acquired at least one customer as a result of their blog.

- It is projected that by 2013, 128 million people in the U.S. will read blogs.
- Businesses who market to businesses with blogs generate 67% more leads than those that do not.
- 61% of online shoppers in the U.S. purchased something based on recommendations from a blog.
- The average person watches 182 videos online monthly.
- Small businesses that blog generate 126% more lead growth than those that don't.
- Reading original content in a blog results in 60% of consumers feeling more positive about a company.
- 90% of consumers find custom content useful and 78% believe that companies who put out content want to build good relationships.
- 68% of consumers interested in a particular brand will likely spend time reading their content.

Telling stats aren't they? Blogging is vital to a company's promotion, whether it is on your own blog, someone blogging about you, or guest blogging on another site.

If you haven't entered the blogosphere, I hope now you're on your way.

Social What?

Social Media puts the "public" into PR and the "market" into marketing.

—Chris Brogan

I'll be the first to admit, social media is like nails on a chalkboard for me. I do love my personal Facebook page and reconnecting with old friends from high school and college. But Twitter, Pinterest, LinkedIn, Google+, Instagram, YouTube... the thought of all this gives me hives.

After CastMedic Designs had been in business for about six months, I realized that I really should have a business presence on social media. I cringed when I subconsciously heard the nails screech across the chalkboard, dreading having to handle it. So, I decided to hire a social media manager;

someone who could just *deal* with social media for me. I let them take over and never looked back.

I've shared a great deal of my business mistakes with you, so here's another one... I should have looked back. Regrettably, I spent thousands of dollars completely letting someone else be my voice, which was not a good idea. I'm not saying you can't have someone do it for you, but it's important that you are involved in what is being posted on your behalf. Social media is a very personal reflection of you and your business, so it is critical to manage it closely.

Now that you know you need to interact in social media and you really should be at least somewhat involved in it, it's time to get started and learn how you can use it to benefit your business and enhance your PR.

Tip[#]*108*
What is it Anyway?

Social Media is about the people! Not about your business. Provide for the people and the people will provide for you.

—Matt Goulart

So, why should you have a presence on social media? What can it really do for your business? A ton! It builds your brand recognition (my top tip for PR). If you are posting good, quality content, it establishes you as an expert in your field. By generating this content, you are likely to attract more people to your site, who could potentially be new customers. You are reinforcing your subject knowledge with your existing followers. Becoming well-known on a particular topic via social media (i.e. being Google-able) also allows you to leverage yourself for media opportunities.

Another important factor of social media is its viral nature. In the blink of an eye you can become a household name. If you don't believe the power of social media, just ask Justin Bieber or Psy of *Gangnam Style* fame, both of whom went viral on YouTube and are now million-dollar brands.

I interviewed Nika Stewart, Founder of GhostTweeting, www.ghosttweeting.com, who shared her thoughts on social media. She said it is important to determine what your message or expertise is, and to be very clear about that message. Every single thing you post on social media has to go with that message. You should always be in alignment with your branding and your message. People lose respect and trust for you if you deviate from your message. Consistency breeds trust and reliability.

Tip #109
Zuckerberg's Baby

Thank you, Mark Zuckerberg, for Facebook. I love it both personally and professionally. With your personal Facebook page you are able to connect and interact with friends and family, and the Facebook Company Page allows you to chat with customers and fans.

Your website is basically the face of your company, while your Facebook Page is a way to interact with your followers.

In terms of getting publicity through Facebook, try searching by using the hashtag (#). It allows you to search topics and keywords in your industry and to determine who else is using them. You should also post with hashtagged keywords so others can find you the same way.

To create your company Facebook Page, go here, www.facebook.com/pages/create.php. Remember to make sure your Facebook cover page is aligned and consistent with your overall branding.

Earlier in the book, I shared ways to find Facebook pages of television shows and radio programs on which you are interested in appearing and how to "like" their pages. Doing this allows you to be aware of guest needs and upcoming story topics through your personal Facebook newsfeed.

MY FAVORITE TIP
Beware of what you post on your personal Facebook page. Before I appeared on Dr. Oz, I had to accept the producer's friend request. She checked me out via my Facebook page before allowing me to appear on the show.

Tip #110
Blue Bird Café

In my confession above, I admitted my initial disdain for most social media. In all honesty, Twitter was the hardest medium for me to embrace. Anyone who knows me knows that tweaking and then tweeting anything I have to say in only 140 characters would not be easy. I forced myself to learn how to use Twitter and I have to admit, it's really fun. I love that you can connect and interact with just about *anybody!*

If you haven't signed up yet, you can create your account at twitter.com/account/new. I recommend that whoever creates your Facebook cover page also create one for your Twitter account. Go to Fiverr, www.fiverr.com, and have both created by the same designer for $10.00, so the covers will be designed consistently. Be sure to also have the designer use the same fonts and theme as your website.

As soon as your Twitter account is created, start interacting with producers and reporters by commenting on their posts and adding your expertise. For example, if a business reporter shares an article they've written about trademarks, I might comment, *As an inventor, I agree.* Start building relationships.

A tweet can be no more than 140 characters and it is recommended to keep tweets down to 124 or fewer so someone can either re-tweet or reply. Also, if you are attaching a link, only 118 characters are allowed in your tweet. Twitter really forces you to hone your message to a short sound bite.

Learn Twitter basics and terminology at support.twitter.com/articles/166337-the-twitter-glossary.

Some helpful strategies from Twitter expert, Nika Stewart, of Ghost Tweeting, www.ghosttweeting.com:

- Be specific about your message/expertise.
- Every single post has to go with that message.
- Always be in alignment with your branding.
- Post often because people don't always see your tweets.
- Studies recommend tweeting at least 23 times per day.
- More is better with Twitter.

A helpful feature on Twitter is the ability to create lists. These can be used to keep track of journalists and find out what's important to them and what they are talking about. Not sure how to set that up? Go to support.twitter.com/entries/76460-how-to-use-twitter-lists for step-by-step instructions.

There is a great tool available to help find influencers on Twitter called Muck Rack at www.muckrack.com. This free site allows you to search for journalists by their publication or their subject matter. There are thousands of journalists who can be found on Muck Rack. Entering the "newsroom" allows you to see what is trending on Twitter at that moment and which journalists are tweeting about it. They also send out the Muck Rack Daily in an email, which analyzes what journalists are saying and keeps you informed on current hot topics and trends.

Twellow, www.twellow.com, is the Yellow Pages of Twitter. It's free to register. There are over 3,000 categories to choose from to find people on Twitter. You can search "reporters," "journalists," "news producers," etc.

One last awesome tool with regards to Twitter is Tweeted Times, www.tweetedtimes.com. This site is basically a real-time newspaper created for you, based on your Twitter account. It aggregates news in your Twitter stream and ranks everything by popularity. You can also "favorite" other people's newspapers and follow them. Reading this newspaper is a great way to keep up with producers and/or their shows, journalists, and publications. If you want to know what anyone is tweeting about or what is important to them, read their Tweeted Times.

EXPERT TIP

Show Twitter love to the people you want to have notice you. Find freelance writers and journalists and share their information with your audience. Go beyond the RT (re-tweet). Comment and tell your audience why they should follow this person. The journalist will naturally notice you when you do these things. ~ Nika Stewart, GhostTweeting, www.ghosttweeting.com.

*** My Fun Twitter Encounter—It was early in my Twitter education, and I was still experimenting and fumbling my way through it. I would usually grab my laptop in the evening and just read tweets to see how it worked. It happened to be the evening of Easter Sunday, all the family had gone home, and I was scrolling around on Twitter.

Because of the type of products I have, I follow the accessories director of Marie Claire magazine, who is certified with the blue check on Twitter (in layman's terms, that means he is someone very important). That evening he tweeted, "Anyone make anything good for Easter dinner?" Well yes, in fact I had! I had made my grandmother's recipe of ham wrapped in bread dough. I happened to have taken a photograph of it before we ate, so I shared it with him. I replied with the photo, and we interacted a bit. Another evening soon thereafter he posted something else about food and dining out and then another evening something else. I joked that he could be a New York City food critic.

A few weeks later, I was planning a trip to New York to meet up with a group of entrepreneurial women. I was tasked to find a restaurant for us to have dinner. I thought, "Aha! My Twitter 'friend,' the editor at Marie Claire eats out all the time in New York. I'll ask him." I sent him a tweet, and he kindly responded with a restaurant suggestion. I tried to reserve a table, but the restaurant was booked solid, a month out. I went back to him and asked for another suggestion. When he replied, he was surprised we couldn't get in that far out, he included the restaurant's Twitter handle in the response, so they got the tweet as well. The restaurant must have assumed I was an important connection of his, because they contacted me immediately and arranged for our table of ten at peak dinner hour, on the date I had requested. The ladies thought I was a rock star for getting us into this top rated restaurant.

Behold the power of Twitter! ~ I was an A-List Celebrity… for one night.

Tip # *111*
Pin-It

Pinterest is such a fun form of social media. You find products, ideas, and themes you love and save them on boards and share with people. It's like your very own *Oprah's List* of your favorite things. Pinterest is all about pictures, so it's the perfect forum to visually share what moves you.

Just like all the other social media outlets, your Pinterest boards are not just about self-promotion, but sharing what you enjoy and what inspires you.

If you're not on Pinterest yet, get started here: <u>pinterest. com/join</u>.

What can you pin about your company to inspire others? With CastMedic Designs, we've pinned our products on specific boards, but we have also created other boards such as:

- Get Well Soon
- Comfort Foods
- Laughs: The Best Medicine
- Treat Your Feet
- Broken Bones & Surgery
- Sexy But Comfy Shoes

You can see from this list how all of these items are associated with medical boot fashions and injury, but not specific to our company and our products.

Having doubts about creating a Pinterest account? Over 70 million people are now using Pinterest regularly. According to an article posted on www.readwrite.com, Pinterest is currently the fastest growing social network, and it draws 41% of the e-commerce market compared to Facebook's 37%.

Want to build PR on Pinterest? Create a board and pin articles from bloggers or journalists who cover your topics. You should also pin articles written about you because this publicity helps the journalist gain additional exposure as well. Journalists are able to determine who is driving traffic to their site, so this extra effort will help you in establishing a relationship with the journalist.

Another way to get to know journalists and their interests is to focus on what they pin on Pinterest. Comment, re-pin, and "like" their posts to start building relationships.

The underlying theme of search engine optimization (SEO) has been highlighted throughout the book, and keyword optimization is important on Pinterest as well. When pinning, change the description of things you post to include your keywords. Take advantage of any Internet presence that is available to drive people to your website.

EXPERT TIP

This might seem counterintuitive because Pinterest is all about "pinning" items that you are interested in and that inspire you, but if you are using Pinterest to grow your brand or business, you should set up the majority of your Pinterest boards to reflect the interests of your ideal client/target audience, not your own. That way, if someone arrives at your boards on Pinterest and they see content that is relevant to them, they are more likely to follow you.

—**Andreea Ayers,** Launch Grow Joy,
www.launchgrowjoy.com.

Tip # *112*
Freeze-Frame

My kids have been on Instagram for what seems like forever. According to my teenage daughter, they switched, "when the parents took over Facebook." Tweens and teens have been posting their photos, commenting, and sharing for years. Who would have guessed what a great business resource it would become?

Instagram is basically the visual Twitter. It's a free application to instantly share your photos with followers. As with Pinterest, because it is photo-based, it gives a visual, personal view of what inspires you and your business as well as creating a connection to your brand.

I recently read that over 350 million images are shared daily on social media. If you are a product-based business, have a business with visuals, or can share your brand via photos, you should be on Instagram.

By posting photos and using specific hashtags to describe the pictures, you will attract new followers with similar interests.

As an Instagram newbie, I sought out the advice of Instagram Expert, Sue B. Zimmerman of Insta-Results, www.suebzimmerman.com. She recommended establishing what the top 30 hashtags (keywords) are in your industry and following those hashtagged words.

The website *Tags for Likes* lists the most popular hashtags on Instagram, www.tagsforlikes.com.

You can also search to see if particular journalists are using Instagram, then follow them, and "like" what they are posting.

Determine who influences you, (people who inspire you), who the thought leaders in your industry are, the experts in your field, and particularly the journalists in whom you are interested and follow them. You will also want to repost their photos, which is similar to the re-tweet in Twitter. This sharing is how you build relationships in Instagram.

EXPERT TIP

#InstagramGalTIP – Use the "CLEEP" strategy. Be sure to always hashtag: Categories, Locations, Emotions, Events, Products.

—**Sue B Zimmerman,** The Insta-Gal,
www.subzimmerman.com.

Tip # *113*
Are You Linked In?

LinkedIn is probably the most underutilized medium of social media. It is geared strictly towards business and professional networking. Over 225 million people on LinkedIn are there specifically to connect with other business people. Imagine the network you can create.

To register with LinkedIn go to www.linkedin.com/reg/signup. The most important aspect of LinkedIn is to create a profile that stands out. Use your best headshot. Fill out your profile completely and dynamically by including links and videos.

Your LinkedIn profile is basically your sales page, so make sure you are impressing anyone who stops by to check you out. Feel free to view mine as an example and connect with me at www.linkedin.com/in/ChristinaDaves.

Because LinkedIn is a professional site, it's a smart way to connect with people in the media. Remember what I've been saying throughout this book, journalists need you as much as you need them. If you are a good, credible source, why wouldn't they connect with you? I always connect via LinkedIn with anyone in the media who has either reached out to me or with whom I have connected elsewhere.

I have an impressive lineup of connections including producers, editors, freelance writers, radio hosts, and bloggers. Through the regular LinkedIn membership, which is free, you cannot invite people to connect with you unless you already have a relationship or a mutual connection. But once you start building your following, you can generally find someone to connect you to your targets. When I interviewed Josh Turner of Linked University, www.linkeduniversity.com, he taught us another way to connect with members of the media via LinkedIn. He recommends finding a LinkedIn group of which they are a member, joining the same group, then connecting from there.

There are benefits to having a paid or premium membership to LinkedIn, including being able to send InMail (basically a connection request) to anyone on LinkedIn and inviting them to connect. LinkedIn offers tiered plans with pricing based on the number of InMails you are permitted to send. Obviously, the more you pay, the more you can send, www.linkedin.com/static?key=welcome_premium. LinkedIn often sends out free coupon codes for a month of premium membership, so you might want to hold out for the coupon and give it a try for free.

Once connected with someone from the media, I send a message or email thanking them for the connection. Depending on the outlet, I might share my expertise and explain how we could work together in the future.

MY FAVORITE TIP
In less than one year, I connected with over 500 people on LinkedIn. Connect with every businessperson you come in contact with. You never know with whom they might be connected that could help you in the future.

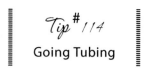

Tip #114
Going Tubing

YouTube is an online video-sharing site that allows you to reach your audience through video. It's the closest thing online to an actual face-to-face encounter. Posting videos on YouTube is similar to putting commercials on TV for free.

You are then able to share these videos with reporters and bloggers. If you're providing valuable content, there is the possibility a blogger might just put your entire video on their site. Either way, it's a good way to open a dialogue with a reporter or blogger.

Some YouTube statistics from their site, www.youtube. com:

- More than 1 billion unique users visit YouTube each month.
- Over 6 billion hours of video are watched each month on YouTube—that's almost an hour for every person on Earth, and 50% more than last year.
- 100 hours of video are uploaded to YouTube every minute.
- YouTube is localized in 56 countries and across 61 languages.
- According to Nielsen, YouTube reaches more US adults ages 18-34 than any cable network.

Think you can't make a video? Do you have an iPhone or comparable smartphone device? They all have pretty decent video capability. Videos are powerful, so it's important to start posting and sharing them yourself.

Not sure what to post? Talk about your expertise. Share other media exposure you've received. Do a video describing your product or service. I filmed a basic "How To" video with our home video camera, in our family room, demonstrating how to use CastMedic Designs' products. That video has over 3,000 views.

EXPERT TIP

Video doesn't need to be perfect, it needs to be powerful. Powerful video doesn't come from expensive equipment, flashy lights, or fancy graphics. Powerful video comes from you. When you are starting out with video keep it simple, keep it focused, keep it powerful. All you need is a camera, mic, and your passion. Your goal is to make your viewer feel emotion. That emotion is not only what compels your customers to action, but it also shows TV casting producers that you make good television. You move the casting producer, you'll be chosen very quickly.

—**Martin Skibosh**, Hollywood Video Editor (Wipe-Out and Beyond Scared Straight), e3studios.tv.

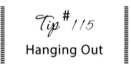

Tip # *115*

Hanging Out

With over 500 million registered users, Google+ is now the 2nd largest social media network having passed Twitter, but still behind Facebook.

Get started by creating your Google+ profile at plus. google.com. This profile set-up is similar to the other social media sites. You'll want to add your headshot and have whoever created the cover pages for Facebook and Twitter, design one for your Google+ account.

Google+ is unique because you can organize people you follow and people who follow you, in what they call "circles." All posts, unless specific to a unique group, for example sharing a family photograph, should be posted to the Google+

Public circle. You can then decide if you want to send a post specifically to a group of circles and then notify them of the post via the e-mail setting.

I recommend separating your personal contacts from business contacts by dividing your contacts into specific circles. For example, I have:

- Friends & Family
- Business Contacts
- Influencers
- Brands
- PR Alert
- Other (you can always move them to a different circle)

This informative short video shows you how Google+ circles work, www.google.com/+/learnmore/circles.

I was extremely fortunate to interview Ronnie Bincer, The Hangout Helper, www.thehangouthelper.com, who is a Google+ guru with over 60,000 people in his circles. He explained how we can use Google+ to connect with the media.

You can find a journalist or influencer in your industry and put them in a specific Google+ circle category you have created. Even if they do not reciprocate, you'll have access to all of their posts and can comment or share. By including them in your circles, you can discover what they are writing about and where you might be able to fit in.

In time, as you build relationships with journalists in your circle, you can send them a direct message and ask them if they would like to opt-in to your circle and be alerted directly when you have newsworthy information to share. You would address a post to the Public circle and also to your specific opt-in circle so the journalist would be notified when you share a newsworthy post (in case they missed it on the main feed).

Another feature for finding and interacting with others on Google+ is communities, a gathering place for like-minded people who care about a specific topic. These are people interested in sharing their information and hearing what you have to say. You can find communities based on your business, hobbies, media outlets, or even similar communities where journalists might be members. You can comment on or share posts and start interacting with people in communities. You can search out communities based on keywords or Google+ will recommend communities based on those you have in your circles. Learn more at www.google.com/+/learnmore/communities.

Google+ also uses hashtags which are important for search engine optimization (SEO). People search topics based on hashtags. Keep in mind Google+ is part of Google, so they'll be indexing and ranking content of their own social network. If you are starting or participating in active conversations using hashtags, that can only help build your SEO.

EXPERT TIP

As you gain following and influence on Google+, that power spreads exponentially. That's because the personalizing effect can reach into your extended network (the Google contacts of the people who are your Google contacts). That means that if one person who has 10,000 Google+ followers (and/or other Google contacts, such as people in her Gmail contacts) follows you, you've gained the ability to potentially influence the search of not just

one, but 10,000 other people, most of whom don't even know you exist!

> —**Mark Traphagan**, Director of Digital Outreach for Virante Inc., and one of the original Google+ users. He has over 63,000 people in his circles.

Tip # 116
80/20 Rule

A standard rule of thumb for social media is to post good content or information about others 80 percent of the time, and then it's acceptable to self-promote the other 20 percent.

Etc.

I Think I Can! I Think I Can!

Patience, persistence and perspiration make an unbeatable combination for success.

—Napoleon Hill, Author

*P*lease don't give up if you don't hear back on your first try. PR is a lesson in patience and perseverance. Prepare yourself for "no," but don't let it deter you. Keep trying different contacts and angles— always stay professional and on-topic—eventually, you will hear that "yes," and the rewards will be outstanding. I hear about 100 "no's" for every "yes." But when I get a "yes," it is usually a big one!

Just because you haven't gotten a response from someone to whom you are submitting, don't give up. Remember, they are receiving hundreds of submissions every single day. If you are submitting relevant, timely information, continue to do so. You never know when that reporter or producer is going to need your information or will want to do a story on your topic. Your goal is to be the one they think of when they are looking for timely, quality information on a particular topic. It's all about building relationships.

MY FAVORITE TIP

Why you shouldn't give up… I have a contact at a national television show to whom I sent periodic story ideas for an entire year before she responded to one that she thought was a good idea.

Tip #*118*
What's the Worst That Can Happen?

Your mountain is waiting, So… get on your way!"
—Dr. Seuss

A mantra I have lived my life by and have also raised my children with is, "Just ask! What's the worst they can say?" Send that story idea. Write that email. Call that producer. What is the worst that can happen? They say, "No, thank you." So you didn't get on when you wanted. The first "no" is the worst. They do get easier. And remember, that "no" is actually the start of a relationship.

I can't tell you how many incredible things have happened in my life just because I asked! Take a look at Expert's Corner, www.prforanyone.com/experts-corner, where amazing people volunteered their time to share their knowledge. I was able to interview media industry elite, just by asking. Both professionally and personally, my life is full of proof that great things can happen when I simply ask for them. What's the worst anyone can say?

Tip # *119*
"No" Or "Not Now"?

One's best success comes after their greatest disappointments.

—Henry Ward Beecher

Handling your own PR takes a thick skin. You can't take no response or "no" personally. Journalists receive hundreds of submissions every single day. If you hear back and it's a "no," thank them for their consideration and keep them as an active contact. When something else comes up or you have another idea, send it to them. Time and time again, people who work in the media have told me that as long as you are providing fresh content, they want to see it.

I'll share a few personal stories about hearing "no" and how they really were a "not now."

I met a radio host at an event, gave him an idea, and he said, "That's not really what we cover." I nicely asked if I could put together a formal idea for the show and send it in. He liked what I sent, booked me on the show, and I received the most amazing complement: the host was so engaged in our conversation that he missed a commercial break. He actually phoned me after the interview and said in twenty years of interviewing celebrities, authors, and prominent guests, he had never been so engrossed in an interview that he missed a scheduled break.

Another "not now" was submitting story ideas to a *Today Show* producer for a year (all timely, potentially good stories), before she responded and told me her thoughts on my latest idea. Remember, you want to build relationships so the media will eventually just come to you.

Tip [#] *120*

Drip, Drip, Drip

About half of what separates successful entrepreneurs from the non-successful ones is pure perseverance.

—Steve Jobs

If you have something pertinent or newsworthy to share, follow-up with anyone in the media you have made contact with. You never know who might be interested. Repeatedly, people in the media whom I've interviewed have told me that it's okay to continue to submit ideas. Just don't continue to submit the same idea to the same journalist. Odds are if they didn't respond, they're not interested in that particular idea or perhaps just not at that moment. However, submitting a new idea is fine and is welcomed.

Tip # 121
It's All About Them

Talk to someone about themselves and they'll listen for hours.

—Dale Carnegie

Remember that you are trying to build relationships with the media. Avoid sending emails that appear to be spam. Always address an email personally with, "Dear John" or "Dear Mr. Smith." Let them know that you read their magazine or watch their show and where you see a fit. Talk about them before you talk about you. Let them know how you can help them. Odds are you probably won't get booked or have a story written your first time out of the gate. There's a good chance you won't even get a response, but if you do, you've started your relationship with that person.

Tip # 122
Make a Plan

Make an annual PR plan broken down by month that includes who you are going to submit ideas to and when. Here are some suggestions of what to include:

- Every day—Review and respond to the free media query services and check their Twitter sites.
- 1st and 15th - check all the talk shows for pertinent topics and guest suggestions. Do you fit? Send in an

idea. (Ellen, www.ellentv.com/be-on-the-show, Steve Harvey, www.steveharveytv.com/be-on-the-show, Rachael Ray, www.rachaelrayshow.com/show-info/be_on_the_show)

- Go through the editorial calendars of the magazines you feel are a good fit and make note of when you need to send your idea. Put dates on your calendar so you don't miss an opportunity.

- If you are located in or near New York City, Los Angeles, or Chicago and are interested in television opportunities, include Craig's List in this plan.

- Look through the "non-traditional" calendar and determine what holidays you can align with your business and come up with unique story ideas and mark your calendar.

Tip # *123*

Nice to Meet You

Build relationships with anyone you work with in the media. When someone does respond to your idea, whether it's a yes or no, you now have a relationship to foster with that media contact. Media people move around all the time. Once you have a relationship with a writer or producer, stay in touch. They might move to another publication or program that fits with your business or product, and they can use you in the future.

Tip # *124*

Connect Connect Connect

If you want to win at networking, don't keep score.
—Harvey Mackay

I am a firm believer in networking and connecting. Stay connected with anyone and everyone you meet in business. My social media go-to for connecting is LinkedIn. If I have a phone conversation with someone, meet someone at an event, or am mutually introduced, afterward I will immediately connect with them on LinkedIn. If they aren't on LinkedIn but I have their contact information, I add them to my address book. PR is all about who you know, and often times, who they know.

Tip # *125*

Thank You Very Much

The smallest act of kindness is worth more than the grandest intention.

—Oscar Wilde

Always send a handwritten thank you note after you appear on any show or in a publication. Do not use email. Go the extra step and handwrite a note. I always send a note on a card with my company logo.

MY FAVORITE TIP

An inexpensive resource for custom stationery is Vista Print, www.vistaprint.com. They regularly have specials, so I joined their mailing list and waited for a great deal and then stocked up.

Tip # *126*
Meet the Media

There are often paid opportunities to attend a "meet the media" event and actually interact with journalists.

Steve Harrison runs a multi-day event in New York City two times a year called National Publicity Summit, www.nationalpublicitysummit.com. Although pricey, he provides access to over 100 journalists in a speed-dating format. The line-up usually includes major network shows such as, the *Today Show, Good Morning America, CNBC,* as well as major publications including, *O Magazine* and *Family Circle* and also regional television shows, magazines, radio stations, as well as freelance writers. They also provide training before and after the summit so attendees are prepared to meet the journalists and employ tools for the follow up.

Genesis Group, based in New York, currently holds monthly "Meet the Media" events in several cities including New York, Washington, D.C., and Seattle. They are looking to expand to other cities as well. These events are under $100 and limited to 50 attendees and have a small panel of three to five media experts. The panels feature two to three top media outlets such as, the *Today Show, Good Morning America, CNBC,* the *Huffington Post, Redbook,* and *Inc.,* along with a PR professional. Attendees can interact with the outlets during a question and answer session held at the end of the event, www. meetup.com/Meet-the-Media.

A Fond Farewell

Perhaps in retrospect, I should be thanking Richard for discovering there was a faux fur shortage in China. Without that, I probably wouldn't be here. I probably would have hired a publicist and gone that route, and who knows what would have happened. I might have written this book with a different introduction about my publicist, "Richard."

I didn't share this story earlier in the book but when I was having such great success handling my own PR, I thought I should hire a professional to take over for me. My theory was that if I was getting such great coverage on my own, imagine what someone who really knew what they were doing could do? I shelled out $1500 and got... absolutely nothing. In fact, other than a few emails from an assistant, I never heard from them again. But in that same month, I got myself booked on *Dr. Oz*, *FOX5* in D.C. and was featured in both *Parenting* and *Smart CEO* magazines.

It was at this moment that teaching other small business owners and entrepreneurs about publicity became my labor of love. I learned from my mistakes and moved past heartache to create a successful business.

I wish you luck in your endeavors and hope you found my information, and what my amazing friends, mentors, and industry experts shared with you, helpful. There is no doubt in my mind that if you implement these practices, you will have success.

And don't forget, I'm still on this journey with you. I am constantly promoting CastMedic Designs and now PR for Anyone.™ I still haven't reached my big dream of a national morning show such as, *Today* or *Good Morning America,* but I'm on my way building relationships with those producers. There's not a doubt in my mind should Natalie Morales have a bunion removed (she's a big runner), they will be contacting me to make her look great on-air. I will continue to submit story ideas as well, and hopefully one day soon, one will fit. I always keep Elizabeth Lombardo in the back of my mind. She tried for two years before the *Today Show* saw something they liked and had her on the show.

Stay passionate. Be persistent (but be nice about it). Start building relationships with people in the media. Look at all the people I was able to interview both on-camera for Expert's Corner on the website and for this book. These relationships were all built in less than 18 months from product launch to book completion.

You can do it too!

Connect with me and please stay in touch. I'd love to hear if anything you implemented as a result of this book brought you great results.

Twitter - www.twitter.com/prforanyone
Facebook - www.facebook.com/prforanyone.com
LinkedIn - www.linkedin.com/in/ChristinaDaves
Google+ - plus.google.com/109392149361127461028/
posts

It is never too late to be what you might have been.

—George Eliot

About the Author

Christina Daves is a native Washingtonian. She attended Virginia Tech where she received a Bachelor of Arts in both Political Science and German. She resides in the suburbs of Virginia outside of Washington, D.C. with her husband and two children.

Christina's career as a serial entrepreneur debuted with an event planning company she started with two close friends. Their signature events, multi-stage outdoor concerts held in D.C., drew up to 10,000 attendees. The company's big claim-to-fame was booking the then unknown Dave Mathews Band for a concert at a beach bar in Delaware.

A few years later, Christina met her husband and decided that partying for a living was not conducive to married life or starting a family. So off she went to work for the father of one of her partners, still in the planning business, but a toned down version that involved learning about utilizing land for real estate development rather than rock 'n roll.

Shortly after Christina learned the ropes, her mentor retired and she was able to use her newfound knowledge to start a niche business performing feasibility studies for data centers. Fortunately, she lived in the area where AOL is headquartered. Their datacenter explosion kept her busy for many years.

During that time, Christina and her husband moved to the outer suburbs where you find a large number of houses but no businesses established yet. It was in 2002 that the datacenter industry really started slowing down. Always the entrepreneur and observing the need for retail in her area, Christina and her best friend decided to try their hands at a brick and mortar retail store.

With no experience in retail, other than knowing what kinds of things she and her friend liked to buy, they rented and renovated an historic house and stocked it with merchandise. The house was once a Civil War nursing station, believed to be haunted by a colonel who died there. The colonel must have approved of their retail store, Details for the Home, because he's never interfered and it remains a successful business today.

After having the time of her life running Details, Christina was torn over the demands of a retail store and having two very active children. Difficult as it was, she opted to retire from the retail industry and sold her share of the store back to her best friend.

Christina spent 2009 to 2010 at home with her children, not working. She was pulling her hair out not having a business to run. Fortunately, in the summer of 2010, an unfortunate accident led to a brilliant business idea. Christina broke her foot and was placed in an ugly medical walking boot the day before heading to New York City, Fashion Capital of the

World. Finding nothing available on the market to dress it up, she launched CastMedic Designs, a company that designs and manufacturers fashion-forward accessories, allowing anyone stuck in a medical boot to introduce fun and fashion into their healing wardrobe.

She officially launched CastMedic Designs in early 2012. During that first year, she was named one of the *Leading Moms in Business* by Startup Nation. Christina was also chosen as *Steve's Top Inventor* during an inventor's competition on the nationally syndicated *Steve Harvey Show*. She is currently nominated for *2013 Woman Inventor of the Year* by WomenInventorz Network.

Christina's success in independently publicizing CastMedic Designs resulted in her appearing in over 50 media outlets in one year. She has even accessorized a few famous broken bones by outfitting celebrities with medical boot bling.

These amazing accomplishments led her to found PR for Anyone,™ an online resource site for small business owners, entrepreneurs, and authors. PR for Anyone™ provides resources and programs to help users easily and effectively generate their own publicity. Her passion is sharing her experiences with other small business owners and entrepreneurs to help them create their own PR success.

You can reach her directly at christina@prfornayone.com.
Websites:
www.healinstyle.com
www.thehealingpoweroffashion.com
www.prforanyone.com
www.christinadaves.com

Resources

About the Author

www.healinstyle.com
www.thehealingpoweroffashion.com
www.prforanyone.com
www.christinadaves.com
www.facebook.com/prforanyone
www.twitter.com/PRforAnyone
www.prforanyone.com/experts-corner
www.prforanyone.com/shop
www.linkedin.com/in/ChristinaDaves

Website Information

www.godaddy.com
www.retailmenot.com
www.top10bestwebsitebuilders.com

Graphic Information

www.elance.com

www.odesk.com

www.99designs.com

www.craigslist.com

www.fiverr.com

Printing Resources

www.gotprint.com

www.vistaprint.com

Clipping Services

www.burrellesluce.com

us.cision.com/media-monitoring/media-monitoring-overview.asp

www.vocus.com/advanced-pr/monitor

www.cyberalert.com

webclipping.com

www.google.com/alerts

en.mention.net

www.talkwalker.com/alerts

Public Speaking

www.toastmasters.org

www.nsaspeaker.org

Miscellaneous People Cited

www.shopatdetails.com

www.monicatrue.com

www.steveolsher.com

www.glutenfreeschool.com

www.thenofearzone.com

www.gatorrons.com

www.coachgay.com

www.psibands.com

www.nataliemashaal.com

www.acerbicfilm.com

www.linkeduniversity.com

www.shawnetv.com

www.iSeeMeOnTV.com

www.Entreprenette.com

e3studios.tv

www.launchgrowjoy.com

www.suebzimmerman.com

Press Release Examples

service.prweb.com/who-uses-it/examples-by-industry

www.ereleases.com/i/BigPressReleaseBook.pdf

Paid Press Release Services

www.prnewswire.com

www.ereleases.com

www.prweb.com

Free Press Release Services

www.prlog.org

www.free-press-release.com

www.onlineprnews.com

www.newswiretoday.com

www.openpr.com

Free Media Query Sites

www.helpareporterout.com
www.mediadiplomat.com
www.publiseek.com
www.sourcebottle.com
www.pitchrate.com
www.profnetconnect.com

Free Media Query Twitter Sites

twitter.com/helpareporter
twitter.com/ProfNet
twitter.com/pitchrate
twitter.com/mediadiplomat
twitter.com/Publiseek
twitter.com/sourcebottle
www.experttweet.com

Free Media Query Facebook Pages

www.facebook.com/HelpAReporter
www.facebook.com/ProfNetOnFB
www.facebook.com/PitchRate
www.facebook.com/mediadiplomat
www.facebook.com/publiseek
www.facebook.com/sourcebottle

How to Find the Media

www.contactanycelebrity.com
www.mediabistro.com
www.mediabistro.com/mastheads
www.mastheadsonline.blogspot.com
www.mondotimes.com

Fee Based Media Resources

www.vocus.com/software/#publicity
us.cision.com/media-database/media-database-overview.asp
www.gebbieinc.com/prices.htm
www.easymedialist.com

Trade publications

www.webwire.com/IndustryList.asp

Freelancing Information

www.writersmarket.com

Newspapers

www.usnpl.com

Contact Information on Daytime Shows

www.ellentv.com/be-on-the-show
www.steveharveytv.com/be-on-the-show
www.rachaelrayshow.com/show-info/be-on-the-show
www.facebook.com/ellentv
www.facebook.com/SteveHarveytv
www.facebook.com/katieshow
www.facebook.com/TheRachaelRayShow

Airline Magazines

enroute.aircanada.com
www.openskiesmagazine.com
www.bauermedia.co.nz/Magazines/kiaora-air-new-zealand-inflight-magazine.htm
deltaskymag.delta.com
www.freemagazines.co.za/index.php/our-magazines/indwe

www.voyagermagazine.com.au/current-issue/voyager-magazine

www.cebusmile.com

www.bauer-media.com.au/qantas_the_australian_way.htm

holland-herald.com

www.lhm-lounge.de

www.airtranmagazine.com

www.ryanair.com/en/inflightmagazine

deltaskymag.delta.com

www.hemispheresmagazine.com

www.spiritmag.com

hub.aa.com/en/aw/americanway

www.usairwaysmag.com

hub.aa.com/es/nx/nexos

hub.aa.com/en/cl/celebratedliving

www.hanahou.com

www.privatejourneymagazine.com

www.airtranmagazine.com

Make-Up
www.maccosmetics.com/locator/index.tmpl

New Shows and Television Pilots
www.productionweekly.com

Mass-email program
www.yourmailinglistprovider.com

www.constantcontact.com

Free Radio Queries
www.radioguestlist.com

www.radio-locator.com
radiostationworld.com

Blog Resources
www.Typepad.com
www.Wordpress.com
www.Blogger.com
www.ehow.com
www.copyscape.com
www.business2community.com/become-a-contributor
www.technorati.com

U.S. Government Copyright Laws
www.copyright.gov/title17

Social Media Resources
www.ghosttweeting.com
www.facebook.com/pages/create.php
www.thehangouthelper.com
twitter.com/account/new
support.twitter.com/articles/166337-the-twitter-glossary
support.twitter.com/entries/76460-how-to-use-twitter-lists
www.muckrack.com
Muck Rack Daily
www.twellow.com
www.tweetedtimes.com
pinterest.com/join
www.readwrite.com
www.tagsforlikes.com
www.linkedin.com/reg/signup
www.linkeduniversity.com

www.youtube.com
http://linkd.in/1cQf1x8
plus.google.com
www.google.com/+/learnmore/circles
www.google.com/+/learnmore/communities

Meet the Media Events
www.nationalpublicitysummit.com
www.meetup.com/Meet-the-Media

Connect with PR for Anyone™
Twitter - www.twitter.com/prforanyone
Facebook - www.facebook.com/prforanyone.com
LinkedIn - www.linkedin/in/christinadaves
Google+ - plus.google.com/109392149361127461028/posts

HOW WOULD YOU LIKE TO GET
ON TV, RADIO AND IN PRINT... *FOR FREE?*

PR is all about building relationships and offering those in the media avenues to become familiar with you and your business.

Visit PR for Anyone's PR Shop to find unique resources to help you get free exposure for your business. We'll show you how to:

- Develop and create great ideas to submit to the media.
- Entice the media by luring them with a great "hook."
- Find virtually anyone in the media or allow PR for Anyone™ to do it for you.

PR for Anyone's resources show you how to offer targeted and exciting story ideas and turn yourself into the most valuable go-to source in your industry.

Don't miss these opportunities to gain media exposure for you or your business!

WWW.PRFORANYONE.COM/SHOP